Exhibition of the Kingdom of Heaven to the World

Darrell L. Guder

PRESS

Louisville, Kentucky

Editor: Martha S. Gilliss

Book interior and cover design by Jeanne Williams

First edition

Published by Witherspoon Press
Louisville, Kentucky

Web site address: www.pcusa.org/witherspoonpress

PRINTED IN THE UNITED STATES OF AMERICA

07 08 09 10 11 12 13 14 15 16—10 9 8 7 6 5 4 3 2 1

Library of Congress Cataloging-in-Publication Data

Library of Congress Control Number: 2007929438

Contents

Preface

In this contribution to the Great Ends of the Church series, Dr. Darrell L. Guder opens up the meaning of the sixth Great End, the exhibition of the kingdom of heaven to the world. As he makes clear, it itself is the end—in the sense of *telos* or goal—of the other ones: the proclamation of the gospel for the salvation of humankind; the shelter, nurture, and spiritual fellowship of the children of God; the maintenance of divine worship; the preservation of the truth; and the promotion of social righteousness. It is such, however, not because we "get there" after having perfected the first five. Rather, exactly like the other Great Ends, the exhibition of the kingdom of heaven is a gift of grace that flows through our hearts and souls to reach out to the world to manifest or reflect Christ's presence in the world. By grace through faith we are sent out as missional people to the world, as people whose task it is to exhibit the kingdom of heaven.

However, the true sense of kingship and what it means to participate in the kingdom of heaven are not at all clear today. Dr. Guder claims "that one of our urgent tasks is to rediscover the central message of the kingdom of God in its biblical fullness." This is a challenge for us as westernized Christians because our thinking about the meaning of "kingdom" has been so profoundly shaped by the legacy of Christendom. Moreover, many women (and some men, too) are not entirely comfortable attributing masculine qualities to God. The linkage of maleness with royal rule can easily evoke negative experiences of the misuse of patriarchal power for some. Guder guides us away from these concerns and provides us a more inclusive perspective based on the reality of God as transcending gender. Through a critical analysis of monarchical thinking in relationship to God's reign that is based on Scripture and the confessions by which the church professes its faith, Dr. Guder helps to move our thinking in a new direction. He reminds us that power—or rather our experience of power—is not the appropriate instrument with which to measure the reality of God's sovereign rule. Rather, God's rule and reign are that which express and reveal God's power, which is perfect goodness and holiness. God's power is itself the measure of God's power, which is revealed in the life, death, and resurrection of Jesus Christ.

The missional call of the church to exhibit the kingdom of heaven to the world is inclusive and thus universal, extending throughout the entire world, breaking up all boundaries and turning human assumptions about power upside down. The Spirit blows through congregations, transforming communities of faith into missional disciples who are continuously being renewed and reformed according to the Word of God to carry the ministry of Jesus Christ out into our various workplaces. From the tiniest local congregation to the farthest extents of the inhabited universe, the kingdom of heaven is exhibited "as the sole lordship of Jesus Christ . . . practiced in the cultural and organizational diversity of the global movement of God's Spirit."

The hope expressed in this little book is profound. It begins in the grace of our Lord Jesus Christ, the love of God, and the communion of the Holy Spirit. It draws us into Scripture as the Word of God to us. I invite you all not only to read but also to study and discuss this book in Sunday school, in book groups, on retreats, or in whichever setting best suits you.

The Reverend Martha Schull Gilliss, Ph.D.
Editor, Witherspoon Press
Presbyterian Church (U.S.A.)

Talking about the Kingdom

"The kingdom of heaven" is the theme of the sixth Great End of the church. The phrase itself is one biblical version of a theme that dominates Scripture. It expresses the basic biblical conviction that God is sovereign over all creation and history, past, present, and future. This faith claim, that the Old Testament constantly affirms, culminates in the New Testament in Jesus' message of the kingdom of God. It is a vast and many-faceted theme because ultimately it has to do with who God is and what God does in relationship to every area of life. In the earthly ministry of Jesus, it is the central theme of his proclamation, constantly elaborated in his parables and demonstrated in his acts of power (what John calls "signs"). In the church's proclamation from Pentecost onward, the biblical proclamation of the kingdom of God merges with the Christian confession that Jesus Christ is Lord. This conviction is the foundation for the Christian mission. It is because Jesus announces that "All authority in heaven and on earth has been given to me" (Matt. 18:18), that the disciples can become apostles, obeying the command that then follows in the Great Commission of Matthew's Gospel: "make disciples of all nations" (v. 19). Thus, the "exhibition of the kingdom of heaven to the world" basically defines the church's missional calling and summarizes the first five Great Ends of the Church.

This comprehensive way of relating the biblical message of the kingdom of God to the church's overarching mission may seem strange to some. Over the centuries, the church has understood the theme of the kingdom of God in diverse ways, many of them problematic. A detailed exploration of all the ways the theme has been used in the long history of Western Christianity will not be possible. But it will be important for us to recognize how the theme of the kingdom has been adapted and even compromised in the history of what we now call "Christendom." That term refers to the distinctive way in which Christianity became the official and legally protected religion of Western societies, and how the Christian churches became partners of the state. This is sometimes described as "Constantinianism," referring to the political process initiated by the emperor Constantine in the fourth century. It resulted in the legal "establishment of the Christian religion." "Establishment" describes the process in which the emerging societies of Europe assigned to Christianity the status of the only legally allowed religion. The impact of the legal establishment upon the institutional church was enormous. It benefited from an impressive range of special privileges and rights.

The privileged position of Christianity in Western societies resulted in the gradual "Christianization" of European cultures. This was the process in which every aspect of our political, social, and cultural reality came to be understood as "Christian." It resulted in the conviction that we lived in "Christian countries," and that we were Christians because of where we lived. We counted our years as *anno Domini*—the year of our Lord. Our holidays were Christian "holy days." Church towers dominated the architecture of our villages and towns. Everyone lived within hearing range of church bells. To be European was to be Christian. More subtly, we also assumed that to be Christian meant that one must necessarily be European. The vast majority of the populations on both sides of the North Atlantic still regard their cultures as "Christianized," although there would be little consensus on what "Christian" actually means, and little acknowledgment that the claims or authority of Jesus Christ has anything to do with it.

As that history unfolded over the centuries, the biblical focus on the "kingdom" or the "reign" of God went through profound adaptation. It got entangled with human forms of power, and even violence. The Christian church evolved into a hierarchy modeled on Roman structures of power, with King Jesus gradually taking on the characteristics of the emperor. The bishop of Rome, now called the Pope, claimed to be the "vicar of Christ" ruling over Christendom. Matters were made more complicated by the way that the expansion of Christianity took place in Europe. It often happened "from top down"—rulers became Christian, were publicly baptized, and, as a consequence, everyone in their realms would gradually be drawn into the church and the practices of the faith. When historians examine these processes carefully, it becomes clear that many different factors—political, social, and religious—are interacting.[1]

Theologically, there are indeed questions to be raised about the understanding of the gospel that was at the heart of many "Christianization" processes. If we were to ask at any point during the history of Western Christendom just what "the exhibition of the kingdom of heaven to the world" really meant for the faith and practice of people calling themselves Christians, we would find that the answers would reveal serious levels of distortion, superficiality, and even manipulation of the gospel. This is perhaps nowhere more obvious than in the adaptations made by European Christianity to the structures of power and violence.

Over time, Western monarchies began to claim that they ruled "by divine right." Within a few centuries of Constantine's initiatives to establish Christianity as the religion of the empire, theologians were developing theories of "just war" that were used to validate Christian monarchs' use of violence for political ends. Gradually the political systems of Europe, linked under the spiritual hierarchy of the church and its princes, assumed that somehow the kingdom of heaven and Christianized Europe were, in fact, God's intended kingdom of heaven on earth. To be faithful Christians meant to be submissive subjects. Human laws and God's law were woven into each other. In many places, bishops and cardinals became at the same time princes and rulers, with great power and wealth. Priests were regarded as part of the system of divine–human rule who were to provide their parishioners the means of grace and ensure that they conducted themselves as loyal subjects of divinely appointed rulers. When people advocated doctrines or practices that the church deemed heretical, their condemnation by the church could result in the state's execution of them. By the early nineteenth century, the pastors in Prussia were ordered by the king to monitor all of the public schools to ensure that proper submission to the crown was being taught.

Perhaps no major theme in the biblical testimony has been as distorted or neglected in the course of Christendom than has been this central emphasis on the kingdom of God. There was always critical reaction to such mixtures of human and divine claims to rule. There were renewal movements and prophetic challenges to misrule by so-called "Christian monarchs." There were theological attempts to sort out the differences between God's distinctive kingdom and human kingdoms; Luther's differentiation between the "kingdom on the left hand" and the "kingdom on the right hand" was an especially important and influential attempt to clarify these confusions.

Over against all such claims that earthly governments could represent the kingdom of God there was also the vast and diverse emphasis on the kingdom of God as solely a future hope. Instead of seeing any aspect of human existence as an expression of God's reign, this world with its trials was seen as a "vale of tears" through which humans had to pass to prepare for the coming kingdom. The kingdom of God was the promised future in paradise, when earthly woes would be replaced by divine delights. To pray "Thy kingdom come" was to pray for the return of Christ and the arrival of the New Jerusalem. The Christian life was a process of preparation, of purging, of patient and often painful waiting, of anticipation that everything would one day be different. Medieval mystics pursuing the "beatific vision" of God testified to an understanding of God's reign, which could not be polluted with human systems and claims.

After such a diverse and at times contradictory history, talk about the kingdom has become for Western Christians an especially challenging task! Today, we are coming to terms with the fact that "Christendom is over."[2] The pervasive sense that we live in a Christian society in which it makes sense to talk about the kingdom of God is now being replaced by the sense that we are becoming a post-Christian society in which such talk is strange and irrelevant, although we remain a religious nation in the sense that many citizens claim faith in God. Neither the divine right of kings nor the longing for paradise is a shared assumption of twenty-first-century Christians in North America.

As we look back on the problematic history of Western Christendom, we begin to sense that one of our urgent tasks is to rediscover the central message of the kingdom of God in its biblical fullness. As we do try to accomplish this, we discover that we are profoundly conditioned by "Christendom" thinking, so that is very hard for us to grasp the central thrust of the biblical announcement that "the kingdom of God has come near" (Mark 1:15). That message is difficult for the heirs of Christendom to interpret. We Presbyterians have made a significant confessional commitment by stating that the "exhibition of the kingdom of heaven to the world" is a Great End of the church. What that actually means, however, is not immediately obvious.

Perhaps because of the growing awareness that we are going through a time of sweeping change in Western cultures, the kingdom of God theme has inspired much reflection and writing, especially in the last one hundred years. Many biblical scholars have studied this theme in the context of early Christian witness, and they are helping us to set aside our Christendom lenses and reclaim the central message Jesus proclaimed.[3] The scholarly debate about the mystery and meaning of the kingdom of God continues today with great energy. There are obviously many aspects to this theme, which this brief study will not address. Our aim is to understand what it means for our church to say that its last and summarizing Great End is the "exhibition of the kingdom of heaven to the world." We can only do that as we sort out what has happened to the kingdom theology of the Bible over the centuries of Christendom.

Let us think about the language briefly. For most of us in the early twenty-first century in North America, the idea of a "king" is both well known and remote. We encounter kings in history (including biblical history). When we study our European legacy, we learn about the Pope's coronation of Charlemagne as "Holy Roman Emperor." That tradition of royal rule by divine right was claimed as recently as the coronation of Queen Elizabeth II of England in 1953, when her coronation was carried out jointly by the Archbishop of Canterbury and the Moderator of the Church of Scotland in Westminster Abbey. As a result of that act, she was proclaimed the actual head of the Church of England, continuing the tradition established by Henry VIII when he replaced the Pope with himself in that role. More often today, we encounter kings in fairy tales, in some political traditions, and in popular culture (whether it is "king-size" or "Elvis is king!"). Many Americans are fascinated by the pomp and pageantry of the British monarchy, and we may be a little envious at times of our European cousins who still have royal families.

At the same time, we are less impressed when we see many countries that are ruled undemocratically by varying kinds of strongmen—with titles ranging from "president" to "Führer" to "king." We remember that Western democracies emerged in reaction to centuries of bad experience with monarchs. We fought a revolutionary war in order to free ourselves of the onerous rule of a distant king and government. There is a broad consensus that it is a dangerous thing to concentrate too much power in one person's hands. This conviction profoundly shapes the constitutional law and the structures of the government of the United States.

As North Americans, we really have very little idea about what it would mean to live under a king who had legal power over us. After replacing monarchy with representative government, equipped with the safeguards of the check and balance system, we are suspicious of any claims that some human person has the "divine right" to rule over us—even if that person were a follower of Christ! So, we find that when the Bible uses language about the kingdom of God or of heaven, we have virtually no direct experience that would help us understand what that phrase really means. Based on human history, it would be difficult to point to any episode where a particularly good king would serve us as a model to grasp the "reign of God."

In addition, we are aware today of the importance of using language about both humans and God that does not appear to favor maleness over femaleness. "King" is clearly a male term! For this reason, many today prefer to speak of this theme as "the reign of God," or the "sovereignty of God" (of course, the male Latin word *rex,* which means *king,* is present as the root of both those terms!). Since the *Book of Order* uses the term "kingdom of heaven," we will use "kingdom" as well, but interchangeably with "reign" and "rule."[4] As we use it, however, we must constantly remember that gender is not the primary emphasis of the term, but rather the character, actions, and purposes of the one who holds all rule in his hands.

Even in the world of the Bible, it was not always easy to understand just what was meant when someone spoke of God as "king." There were, obviously, many human kings around as examples of the office—monarchy was the dominant form of political organization in the ancient Mediterranean world. But many of these rulers, perhaps most of them, were not the best model for what God was supposed to be like! In this regard, Israel's history is not that different from the typical story of all humanity. The history of the Jewish kings, narrated in the books of Samuel, Kings, and Chronicles, documents that few of the kings performed well in the eyes of the Lord. There is a real tension in the scriptural records of Israel's monarchy. There are strands that emphasize the divine initiative that established the Davidic line with the promise that it would ultimately lead to the world's submitting to God's rule. There are strands that look upon Israel's desire to move from judges to kings as a regrettable compromise with worldly patterns of authority. The ancient wisdom that power corrupts is amply illustrated by Israel's monarchies. God's Word was not absent during the generations of Israel's monarchies: That Word was heard, often in opposition to the kings, from the lips of prophets. Where God's Word and will were often violated or resisted by those on the thrones of Judea and Israel, the prophets constantly and pointedly proclaimed, "And God says." They addressed God's Word to the challenges of injustice, evil, apostasy, and corruption that afflicted God's people, often because of the machinations of their so-called "divine right" king. Yet, because the monarchy was such a widespread institution, it still ultimately made sense to use the idea of the "king" when the biblical witnesses wanted to speak of God's rule. It was the most available and widely understood image.

If we are going to understand what it means for us, as Presbyterians, to "exhibit the kingdom of heaven to the world," we need to move into the biblical world and learn what this language about "king" and "kingdom" meant then. When the biblical witnesses spoke of God in royal terms, what were they saying? What are the major emphases of the biblical claim that God is king and that we are, in some way, part of God's kingdom or God's reign? And, importantly, how are our understandings of "king," "rule," and "sovereignty" shaped by the complex history of Christendom that so thoroughly conditions us? As we go about this exploration, we will see that human definitions of kings relate only superficially to the royal character and action of God. In fact, there is a sense in which God's way of being the ruler over all becomes itself the model for human rulers—but that's another story.

Notes

1. This fascinating story is well told by Peter Brown in his book *The Rise of Western Christendom: Triumph and Diversity, A.D. 200–1000,* 2nd ed. (Malden, MA: Blackwell Publishers, 2003).

2. Many contemporary theologians address the "end of Christendom" in diverse ways: Karl Barth, Dietrich Bonhoeffer, Lesslie Newbigin, David Bosch, and Douglas John Hall. For brief introductions to the theme, see Lesslie Newbigin, *The Other Side of 1984: Questions for the Churches* (Geneva: World Council of Churches, 1983); David Jacobus Bosch, *Believing in the Future: Toward a Missiology of Western Culture* (Valley Forge, PA: Trinity Press International, 1995).

3. As one example, see Mortimer Arias, *Announcing the Reign of God: Evangelization and the Subversive Memory of Jesus* (Lima, OH: Academic Renewal Press, 2001).

4. "Kingdom of heaven" is the particular usage in the Gospel according to Matthew. Where both Mark and Luke speak of the "kingdom of God," Matthew uses the alternative term "heaven." Most scholars agree that this usage reflects the Jewish sensibility of the Matthean Gospel—the pious Jew of that time preferred not to say the holy name of God out of reverence for that name, but would use various alternative terms. Frequently "heaven" was the code word for God.

Questions for Reflection and Discussion

1. What are some examples of how centuries of Christendom continue to influence the way that our American culture functions today?

2. In what ways do you find the term "kingdom of God" difficult to understand in our present-day world?

3. Would your understanding of the kingdom of God place greater emphasis on the evidence of God's rule in present history or on the kingdom's future coming? Why would you make your emphasis the way you do?

4. In view of the statistical evidence that Americans are a very religious society, why does it make sense to talk about the "end of Christendom"? Or, does it?

5. How does this sixth Great End of the church summarize the first five? Does the author's claim that it does summarize the first five make sense to you?

The Power, Purposefulness, and Goodness of God's Rule

The biblical testimony about God, who God is, and what God does consistently emphasizes, in one way or another, the *power*, the *purposefulness*, and the *goodness* of God. Creation itself is narrated as a great act of God's unique power, making life and matter out of nothing. But the power is not arbitrary. It is not a mere demonstration of celestial superiority. It is purposeful. God is making something very good, as Genesis 1 constantly stresses. God reveals in the act of creation that the very nature of God is purposeful and good. Thus, what God makes will itself demonstrate that goodness. Humans are made "in the image of God," and creation is described as a wonderful garden in which all human needs are met, and where God's goodness is enjoyed.

That purposefulness and goodness are revealed in God's desire to create a world for relationship with himself. The Bible makes that point as it constantly stresses that all creation exists to the "honor and glory of God." To be created in the image of God means that humans are made "God-ward" in their fundamental orientation—they are made to know, hear, interact with, and obey their Creator. Prayer is the expression of humanity's true creaturely nature. In the wonderful imagery of Genesis 3, the man and the woman walk with God in the cool of the evening. Thus, all of creation carries the stamp of God's creative power, purpose, and goodness.

The biblical confession that God made all things, and that God continues to provide for all things, is a statement about the character of God's rule. Without using the language of "kingdom," our Reformed confessions emphasize this power and purposefulness as essential aspects of our doctrine of God. In its exposition of the Apostles' Creed, The Heidelberg Catechism describes the character and actions of God as Creator and Provider:

Q. 26. What do you believe when you say: "I believe in God the Father Almighty, Maker of heaven and earth"?

A. That the eternal Father of our Lord Jesus Christ, who out of nothing created heaven and earth with all that is in them, who also upholds and governs them by his eternal counsel and providence, is for the sake of Christ his Son my God and my Father. I trust in him so completely that I have no doubt that he will provide me with all things necessary for body and soul. Moreover, whatever evil he sends upon me in this troubled life he will turn to my good, for he is able to do it, being almighty God, and is determined to do it, being a faithful Father.[1]

In this confession, we affirm God's act of power in creation: Heaven and earth are the result of his command. But we surround that ascription of God's power with further statements that define that power in a particular way: God upholds and governs; God can be trusted for everything truly needful; God turns troubles to good. The God who is "King of heaven" does not withdraw inside heaven, but engages his creation and gets involved in its story. In his actions, God's goodness is displayed: As our "faithful Father," God provides everything the creation needs. In the story of the first couple in Eden, this is underlined in several ways:

- God kneels down in the mud and forms the first human with his own hands (Gen. 2:7);
- God breathes the very breath of life into the human he has created;
- God creates every dimension of the world as a good place in which to live and work and do God's bidding;
- God gives a special command to the humans (Gen. 1:28–30);
- Having made everything very good, God continues to relate to and be with this creation: God walks with the first couple in the garden in the cool of the day (Gen. 3:8).

In our theological tradition, we have emphasized God's continuing involvement in his creation with the doctrine of providence, which is the theme of the next question in The Heidelberg Catechism:

Q. 27. What do you understand by the providence of God?

A. The almighty and ever-present power of God whereby he still upholds, as it were by his own hand, heaven and earth together with all creatures, and rules in such a way that leaves and grass, rain and drought, fruitful and unfruitful years, food and drink, health and sickness, riches and poverty, and everything else, come to us not by chance but by his fatherly hand."[2]

The powerfulness and goodness of God's power are demonstrated in his providence. God's rule is present in all the twists and turns of history, in all the big and little factors that make up human existence. God is not the distant clock maker who has made and wound up the clock of the universe and now sets it to ticking, while he absents himself. No, God is the Creator who cares deeply for what he has made. This Creator desires to be in community with his creatures, and thus God relates to creation and especially to humanity as a father relating to his children. These are understandings of kingship and rule that are very different from the practices of ancient Middle Eastern monarchs—and modern tyrants! There is, in these fundamental understandings of the character and purposes of God, good news that the psalmists continually lift up in their praise of God.

> The LORD is king, he is robed in majesty. (Ps. 93:1)
> The LORD is king! Let the earth rejoice. (Ps. 97:1)
> The LORD is king; let the peoples tremble! (Ps. 99:1)
> Praise the LORD! O give thanks to the LORD, for he is good;
>   for his steadfast love endures forever. (Ps. 106:1)

The underlying design of all reality is defined by the power, goodness, and purposefulness of the God who wants to be father and mother to his creation. This truly amazing conviction is then expounded in the third question in The Heidelberg Catechism that asks about the impact of our confession that God is Creator and Provider:

Q. 28. What advantage comes from acknowledging God's creation and providence?

A. We learn that we are to be patient in adversity, grateful in the midst of blessing, and to trust our faithful God and

Father for the future, assured that no creature shall separate us from his love, since all creatures are so completely in his hand that without his will they cannot even move.[3]

With this answer, the biblical understanding of God's power departs from all human conceptions of power. The Catechism interprets the biblical story by linking God's power with God's love. This is an amazing claim: God's divine rule, characterized by power, purposefulness, and goodness, is an outworking of God's love for all that he has made. This is ultimately the reason that humans may trust God—it is because God makes it known that his love for his creation guides the practice of his power, defines his purposefulness, and guarantees the goodness of all that he has made. Centering on God's love is the most distinctive claim we can make about the rule of God. This emphasis on God's love drives the Old Testament story and reaches its climax in Jesus' becoming human flesh for the world.

Wherever and however, then, that the "kingdom of heaven" or the "reign of God" is spoken of in the Bible, the reader should always remember that this rule is rooted in love, expressed in power and purposefulness, and displayed in the goodness of all that is. This distinctive reign enables us to trust God as the obvious and proper response to who God is and what God does.

All of this means, then, that the "power" language of the Bible really does not fit with our common understandings of the exercise of power. The distortions of the biblical "kingdom" in the institutions of Western Christendom traditions illustrate how difficult it is for us to engage the biblical word through the lenses of our history. There are enormous differences between the biblical theology of divine rule and the ways that we think about kingship and lordship. Because power and love are inseparable in God's nature and action, God neither coerces human response nor imposes his will arbitrarily. God engages, amazingly, his creatures as partners. God invites them into relationship, makes promises, discloses purpose, and defines what obedience will look like. This is what the biblical theme of covenant is all about.

There are, of course, consequences when humans disobey God. They must experience that their rebellion against God affects every dimension of life and corrupts the essential goodness of God's design. There is judgment because there is sin, which is the human rebellion against God's power, the rejection of his purposes, and the distortion of his goodness. But there is always the possibility of repentance and forgiveness. God does not desire the punishment of his people, and

God constantly reaches out to them, even in their rebellion, to draw them back into relationship with himself. God's rule, rooted in divine love, combines justice and mercy in ways no human system of governance can imitate.

The distinctive character of God's power is made especially clear in the ministry and teaching of Jesus. Jesus' practice of power is not to impress or to coerce. He cannot be tempted to flaunt his power, as Satan attempts to do in the episode in the wilderness. Rather, Jesus' power is expressed in acts of service. His power restores health, casts out demons, raises people to life, breaks down social tabus, and provides for human needs. His power is hidden in the weakness of a human person whose life is entirely committed to demonstrating the purposefulness and goodness of God. Jesus washes the feet of his disciples to teach them how to serve one another. His willingness to go to the cross on behalf of all humanity is the supreme expression of power submitting to divine purposefulness.

This is the model of radically different power, which Jesus passes on to his disciples, and through them to the church. He instructs his disciples that the way power works in his community will be very different from the patterns of the world around them.

> "You know that among the Gentiles those whom they recognize as their rulers lord it over them, and their great ones are tyrants over them. But it is not so among you; but whoever wishes to become great among you must be your servant, and whoever wishes to be first among you must be slave of all. For the Son of Man came not to be served but to serve, and to give his life a ransom for many." (Mark 10:42–45; see Matt. 20:25–28)

The apostles instruct the churches they found to practice this same distinctive power, which is most appropriately expressed in weakness. Jesus is to be their (and our) model for the way they relate to each other and to the world into which God is sending them. Each of them is to "look not to [one's] own interests, but to the interests of others" (Phil. 2:4). Of course, as Easter Christians, they have been transformed by the same power that raised Jesus from the dead, so that they can indeed know "what is the immeasurable greatness of his power for us who believe, according to the working of his great power"—it's the power that "God put . . . to work in Christ when he raised him from the dead. . . ." (Eph. 1:19–20). But we testify to that power as ones who "have this treasure in clay jars, so that it may be made clear that this extraordinary power belongs to God and does not come from us" (2 Cor. 4:7).

When Christians speak, then, of God's sovereignty in creation and history, they often hear the critical question "How does such a God allow so much suffering if God has all that power?" Following the catastrophic tsunamis in Southeast Asia at Christmas 2004, or the devastation of Hurricane Katrina along the Gulf Coast in 2005, many versions of that question could be heard. The biblical witness enables us to respond by saying that God's power is not defined by the powers at work in nature, which can often be cruel and arbitrary. God's power is not in the earthquake or in the storm, but in the voice that speaks to the fleeing Elijah out of the "sound of sheer silence" (1 Kings 19:12). God's power is at work in the weak and the unlikely: in the remnant of Israel that is sent into exile, in the prophets whose voices are not heeded, in the peasant girl who receives astounding news about an approaching birth and accepts God's will for her, and in the infant Jesus whose life is threatened by the human power of Herod. "God's foolishness is wiser than human wisdom, and God's weakness is stronger than human strength" (1 Cor. 1:25).

Notes

1. The Heidelberg Catechism, in *The Book of Confessions*, 4.026.
2. Ibid., 4.027.
3. Ibid., 4.028.

Questions for Reflection and Discussion

1. How does the claim that God is "powerful, purposeful, and good" relate to present-day secular thinking? How might a typical "modern American" react to such a claim?

2. Why would many contemporaries of ours raise questions about the claim that God's love expresses itself in his power, purposefulness, and goodness?

3. What are some biblical examples of the way that God's love pervades his actions toward his creation and even shapes God's practice of justice?

4. Why is it hard for us, as Christians in a late-Christendom setting, to follow Jesus in the way he understood and used his power?

5. What examples could you cite of Christians or Christian groups that have risked following Jesus' radical redefinition of power? How would you describe their importance for us today?

The Human's Place in the Reign of God

According to the ancient stories that make up the beginning chapters of the Bible, the creation of humans was a particular and very purposeful act of God. In the version narrated in Genesis 1, everything else in the world is carefully made and arranged so that, on the sixth day, the human creatures will find a home that is truly good. With the context for human life fully and beautifully created, God then proceeds to make the human person "in his image." The narration in Genesis 2 makes the same basic point when it describes God as the potter who forms the human person out of the dust of the earth and then breathes into it "the breath of life." The creation of the human person is related in important ways to the biblical understanding of the kingdom or reign of God.

There are many dimensions to the theology of the *imago Dei* (the image of God), which are basic to the entire Bible's teaching about what it means to be human. But one of the fundamental meanings of this text has to do with the relationship between God's rule in the world and the role and responsibility of the human creature. The Hebrew word for "image" is related to the terms for "statue" in some of the ancient Near Eastern languages. Particular statues were probably meant: the statues that rulers would set up in their domains to remind their subjects about who was in charge, who had the power, and who was to be obeyed. Even if the king were not there in person, his statue was a constant reminder of his person, his office, and his power. This custom continues today. We think of the many statues of monarchs to be found in countries that have royalty or did in their history, or of the pictures of queens and presidents on postage stamps and coins, or of the photos of heads of state in government offices.

The crucial point, however, is that this word is used about the human creature, both male and female. They are made "in the image of God" to represent God's rule in the world, to the world. To be "in

17

the image of God" does not mean that humans look like God or that God looks like humans. It means that humans are mandated by God to represent to the entire world the goodness and purposefulness of God's creation. They are equipped, therefore, with the capacity to do that. They can make decisions about the conduct of their lives, and their actions will have an effect on all of creation. They are, as the psalmist sings, "a little lower than God," creatures that God has crowned with "glory and honor" (Ps. 8:5).

God gives to the human creatures a divine command, making them distinctive from everything else God created. "Be fruitful and multiply, and fill the earth and subdue it; and have dominion over the fish of the sea and over the birds of the air and over every living thing that moves upon the earth" (Gen. 1:28). God entrusts to his human creatures a share of God's own rule, a responsibility for the created world described as "dominion." This command implies many things. It implies that humans have the capacity to carry out this command. It implies that humans are made with wills, with the ability to make decisions. Humans are designed for obedience to God's command, which means that their decisions are important.

A real danger is that the human, made a little lower than the angels (see Heb. 2:7), might misconstrue the creation command and its shared power as a mandate to exploit or be domineering over all creation. History is tragically full of examples of that abuse of the creation command and its responsibility. The story, as it unfolds in the second creation narrative in Genesis 2, makes it very clear that God intends this shared power to be exercised in a particular way. The earth is described as a beautiful and productive garden that provides everything that God's creatures need for a good existence. The human is assigned the task of the gardener: "The LORD God took the man and put him in the garden of Eden to till it and keep it" (Gen. 2:15). Humans share in God's rule as stewards of the goodness of God's creation. They represent to the world the goodness and purposefulness of God's creation and providence as they carry out their responsibility to maintain this beautiful garden God has made. They demonstrate what it means to be created in the image of God by caring for creation on God's behalf and in terms of God's design. Their share in the reign of God is benevolent, just as God's rule in both creation and providence is benevolent.

The ancient plot of the creation narratives reveals a basic conviction of biblical faith that we have already mentioned above: God's power and purposefulness, although total and unlimited, are not coercive. They are controlled by God's goodness. God's way of exercising rule is not tyrannical or despotic, but caring, loving, focused on the goodness of what he has made and the goodness he intends his creation to enjoy. In order for that loving rule to be possible, it entails the creation of the human with a will, an ability to decide. If God gives humans a command, then they have the option to obey or not to obey. In the same way that God's rule expresses his love and desire for trusting relationships with all creatures, so is the human role in this rule to live lives based on love and trust.

When the humans then choose to disobey God's good command, their relationship to the reign of God is changed but not ended. Their sin distorts all the basic dimensions of their creation and purpose. But they are still the responsible gardeners held accountable for the stewardship of the world committed to them. Now, however, their task is not an easy one. The world reflects the disorder that has entered in through sin, and every aspect of life is somehow affected by this rebellion. The human is still the responsible gardener, but the garden has become a very different place to work. God says to Adam, "Cursed is the ground because of you; in toil you shall eat of it all the days of your life; thorns and thistles it shall bring forth for you; and you shall eat the plants of the field. By the sweat of your face you shall eat bread . . . ." (Gen. 3:17b–19a).

Human life, after Eden, is constantly involved in profound tension. There is the ever-present tension between our identity as people created in the image of God, and people in rebellion against God. We struggle with the knowledge that we are people who are responsible for the good stewardship of the earth and at the same time we are people who exploit the earth's riches for selfish reasons. We sense a deep tension between the way things are and the way that we wish things were: We can use words like "should" and "ought" to express those longings. The fact of this basic tension is a continuing indication of the reign of God and of the image of God placed in the creature. Cast out of Eden, the human senses that life and reality should be different. But we cannot re-create Eden, and we cannot go back to it. These many dimensions of human reality are portrayed in the Bible vividly in the stories of Genesis 1—11, in which the ambivalence of human existence is illustrated over and over again.

God's reign expresses itself, from now on, in many different, and often mysterious ways. While it always expresses, in some way, God's power, purposefulness, and goodness, the emphasis after the Fall shifts. Now God's goodness centers on the healing of this broken creation. This is what "salvation" is all about: healing, restoration to wholeness, reconciliation where there is division. Salvation in this sense of making whole is the purpose of God's actions. God's goodness is demonstrated in his determination that all the nations shall be blessed, and that Abraham should be the father of the nation that will bring about that blessing (see Gen. 12:3). This now becomes both the promise and the reality of God's rule.

God makes clothing for rebellious humans; God protects Cain, the brother–murderer, from destruction and ensures that he will live; God confuses the tongues of the tower builders to rescue them from overweening pride; God lets the floods take their toll of life but preserves a remnant with the inhabitants of the ark. God's mysterious rule (we think again of the exposition of "providence" stated in Questions 26, 27, and 28 of The Heidelberg Catechism) is thus at work in the so-called accidents of nature, in the unlikely twists and turns in people's lives, even in the events in which God's will is clearly opposed. But God does not coerce obedience, and God does not use his power to cow people into submission. God's appeal continues to be that the creature should trust him and obey him: That is still possible!

When Abraham is called to obey God by moving out to a country he does not know, he receives the promise that his seed will become numerous, and this people will be a blessing to all the earth (Gen. 12:1–3; 17:1–8). God's power, purposefulness, and goodness are centered now in the remarkable relationship between God and humanity that the Bible calls "covenant." God makes a covenant, a "partnership agreement," with Abraham and his descendants, an agreement with both promise and mandate. Entering into such a covenant agreement with humans is a further instance of the mysterious way in which God rules. God's reign does not consist of arbitrary interventions and mighty acts of stupefying power. God's rule takes place through the offer of relationship, the promotion of trust, and the insistence on accountability. Humans constantly fail to live up to the conditions of the covenant, and God's sovereign reaction is diverse. Sometimes God lets humans experience the consequences of their own rebellion; sometimes God saves them from their own folly; sometimes God empowers them to act with greater faithfulness and to take bold steps of obedience. God's power and purposefulness may remain obscure in many such turns of the story. But God's reign is never questioned. Through the entire human story, God is working out his purpose of salvation: the healing and restoration of all creation.

God does not compromise his sovereignty in making a covenant with humanity. God created according to the divine vision of the ultimate horizon, and will continue to deal with humanity with this ultimate plan in view. But this does not suggest that we will respond to God without second thought.[1]

So, the mysterious reign of God, so often hidden or apparently mixed with human decision making, continues as the overarching theme of the biblical story. As humans grapple with the sinfulness of their lives and their world, the expectation grows that God will work things out, someday, so that his reign will be perfect and all will obey. God makes promises that point in the direction of such a wonderful transformation. When God covenants with David to establish David's royal line, his promises point toward great events yet to come: an everlasting kingdom of justice and peace (2 Sam. 7:4–17). The prophets anticipate events and confrontations that will draw everything together into God's good purpose. After the failure of so many human kings, the anticipation emerges that God will provide a uniquely called and set-apart person to rule in his name and bring about his purposes. In some strands of the tradition, this expectation is linked with the idea that all of history must first end in a catastrophe, after which God will initiate something new. In other strands, the anticipation is that God will bring about the political primacy of Israel, harking back to the glories of David's reign, and that this human rule will govern all the earth from Zion. In many different ways, the Israelites are told, "The days are surely coming, says the LORD, when I will fulfill the promise I made to the house of Israel and the house of Judah" (Jer. 33:14).

This coming of God's rule in a radically new and transformed way is impressively summarized by the prophet Jeremiah:

> The days are surely coming, says the LORD, when I will make a new covenant with the house of Israel and the house of Judah. It will not be like the covenant that I made with their ancestors when I took them by the hand to bring them out of the land of Egypt—a covenant that they broke, though I was their husband, says the LORD. But this is the covenant that I will make with the house of Israel after those days, says the LORD: I will put my law within them, and I will write it on their hearts; and I will be their God, and they shall be my people. (Jer. 31:31–33)

Note

1. Ken Gnanakan, *Kingdom Concerns: A Biblical Exploration Towards a Theology of Mission* (Bangalore, India: Theological Book Trust, 1989), p. 50.

Questions for Reflection and Discussion

1. How do you react to the author's claim that the divine purpose of the human creature, made in the image of God, is to represent God's good rule to all of creation? How might this emphasis relate today to the concern for the environment?

2. What examples do you see in contemporary culture of the sense of "paradise lost," and in what ways do you see evidence of the search for the restoration of paradise?

3. How do Christians in our society tend to react to secular attempts to reclaim paradise? What problems are linked to such reactions among Christians?

4. What are some common understandings of "salvation" inside and outside the church? How do these understandings relate to the author's emphasis that salvation is about healing and the restoration of wholeness?

5. How does this discussion of salvation relate to your understanding of the first Great End of the church: "the proclamation of the gospel for the salvation of humankind"?

Jesus: Kingdom Proclaimer and King

4

When Jesus begins his earthly ministry, he announces that "the time is fulfilled, and the kingdom of God has come near; repent, and believe in the good news" (Mark 1:15). The kingdom of God then emerges as the dominant theme in Jesus' teaching and preaching, especially in Matthew, Mark, and Luke. Jesus' proclamation of the kingdom draws together all Israel's expectations and longings, and reorients Israel's understanding of the kingdom around what is happening now, in this one person at this time: "The time is fulfilled." What is happening in the life and action of Jesus signals the turning of the ages. God's reign is engaging human history in a new way, drawing together all that God has been doing in and for his creation since Eden. The promises are beginning to be fulfilled. Many of Jesus' signs and wonders point to this newness.

In this in-breaking kingdom, healing ends disease; the social barriers set up by humans are torn down; sins are forgiven; lives of despair are changed into lives of hope; weakness becomes strength; the marginal count as much as the powerful; and children are always welcome. In his teaching, Jesus expounds the purposefulness and goodness of God's creation and rule. He instructs his disciples about the real meaning of the commands not to kill and not to commit adultery: They are really about the rejection of anger and lust (Matt. 5:21–30). Jesus makes concrete and tangible what Jeremiah prophesied when he looked forward to the "new covenant" that God would bring about: "I will put my law within them, and I will write it on their hearts; and I will be their God, and they shall be my people" (Jer. 31:33). The reign of God will be the new relationship with God in which the human rebellion is overcome and replaced with reconciliation, and God's people now live out their creation design. This new relationship will make it possible for God's will to be done.

Under this new covenant, God's purposefulness will be disclosed and acknowledged, and God's goodness will define human reality. This is what Jesus teaches and promises when he instructs his disciples to pray, "Thy will be done, on earth as it is in heaven."

So, as Jesus teaches and demonstrates this in-breaking reign of God, he challenges the interpretations the theology of Israel that have developed over centuries, interpretations that have cushioned and tamed the radical claims of God's sovereignty. In his parables, Jesus teaches his disciples the distinctive patterns of the kingdom's coming. An especially remarkable collection of such parables is in Matthew 13. Here, Jesus equips his disciples for their future ministry as heralds and witnesses of the in-breaking reign of God by telling them about the kingdom of heaven and how it comes. The kingdom of heaven will come about like the growing of plants from seeds. The messengers of the kingdom are to sow that seed, and they are to do so generously. They are to spread the seed of this good message of God's rule in hard, weedy, rocky, shallow soil as well as in fertile ground. The growth that results will be diverse. The seed of the in-breaking reign of God will grow up in all kinds of soil, and some of it will not grow at all. But, because it is God's kingdom whose coming is sure, and because its coming is solely under God's rule, the ultimate harvest will be overwhelming: "a hundredfold, some sixty, some thirty" (Matt. 13:8).

The kingdom that Jesus proclaims is already breaking into human history in his person and action. He himself is the fulfillment of the expectation of that kingdom. This means that it is happening within the ambiguity and contradictions of human reality. The language about the kingdom of heaven is dynamic: It speaks of what God is doing now, what God will continue to do, and what God will ultimately complete. There is a sense both of fulfillment and of new expectation in Jesus' announcement of the kingdom of heaven. His followers are invited into the kingdom now and pray for its coming. Its coming, within the contradictory reality of human history, is always going to be ambiguous—it will often be hard to discern amid all the forms of human rebellion. It is like a field, Jesus says, where good seed was sown, and then, secretly, weeds were sown by God's foes. These seeds sprout and grow together, and the workpeople do not recognize the sadness of this mixture until the plants are grown and the roots intertwined. Jesus instructs them *not* to rush to harvest, which would do great harm to the kingdom that is already here, is nearing, and is yet to come. That harvest task is the Lord's alone, and God will do it in God's time. We are equipped here to know that while the kingdom is emerging, it will often look like a field of good wheat mixed with weeds. Yet humans should not try to sort it out. We are to sow, to water, to nurture, to encourage, but we must leave the harvest judgment to God, who is the Lord of the final harvest.

In the sequence of short parables that completes the collection in Matthew 13, further aspects of the kingdom of heaven are explored. Using the example of a mustard seed, Jesus explains that the kingdom emerges in unlikely ways, comparable to the tiny seed that, once planted, grows and blossoms into a source of blessing for everyone. Here again, human patterns of thought are shown to be inadequate to understand how God is working. Rather then working from human centers of power and influence, God starts with the small and the marginal. Israel and the selection of the disciples, both examples of unlikely choices, are major examples of this strategy. This makes clear that the blessings God brings are the outpouring of his grace and love and not the product of human merit. At the same time, God does disclose enough of his kingdom rule to make it possible for humans to glimpse the wonders of God's kingdom and then to pursue it single-mindedly. It can, therefore, be compared to a treasure or a valuable pearl, for which everything else should be sacrificed. Finally, human attempts to manage the formation of the kingdom will constantly be confounded by God's way of "casting out the net": All kinds of fish will be caught, and only at the end of the age do God's angels separate the evil from the righteous. Human witness to the in-breaking reign of God is not empowered to become the judge of who is "in" and who is "out"—the message is similar to the parable of the mixed field of wheat and weeds. God's rule of power, purposefulness, and goodness is open to all; and those who witness to it are called on to sow the seed on all kinds of soil, to live patiently with the mixed nature of the resulting wheat field, and to focus on God's promise of blessing for all and to seek that treasure without compromise.

In Jesus' day, language about the kingdom evoked all kinds of expectations and responses. Some thought that he was talking about the restoration of David's monarchy. That would mean the end of Roman occupation and the political liberation of the Jews. Others thought he meant an alternative society, withdrawn from all the temptations of the world. Some dismissed his teaching as the rantings of a madman. Others experienced his words and actions as the gift of new life, as happened with Lazarus, Zacchaeus, the adulteress, and Jairus. Jesus' disciples, living with him twenty-four days a day, memorized what he taught and remembered all his actions, not knowing that their discipleship was preparing them for a new vocation: the apostolate. Initially they did not fully understand that following Jesus would ultimately mean being sent by Jesus to carry his message into the world. That would all come together for them from the radically changed perspective of Easter.

When Jesus was finally taken captive, tried, condemned, and executed as a criminal on a Roman cross, the sign over his head reiterated the great theme of the biblical story: Jesus of Nazareth, King of the Jews. But no one was able to grasp how the kingdom of God was erupting in the life of this man. Only in the light of Easter did the early community of followers begin to grasp this remarkable truth: In Jesus the Christ, the kingdom has not only drawn near—it is now here. As we have already emphasized above, Jesus announced his rule to the disciples as he commissioned them to continue the mission: "All authority in heaven and on earth has been given to me. Go therefore and make disciples of all nations . . . ." (Matt. 28:18–19a). "The kingdom now had a name and a face, the name and the face of Jesus."[1]

When the Jewish community, spread around the Mediterranean by the beginning of the first century C.E., translated its Scriptures into Greek, they used the word *kyrios* where the mysterious name of God (YHWH[2]) appeared in Hebrew. This Greek term was used for those who had authority, those who ruled, those who exercised lordship. When the Christian community began to confess its faith in the resurrected Christ, using Greek, they made the astounding and dangerous claim that Jesus Christ is the *kyrios*, the Lord. This phrase, Jesus Christ is Lord, is the church's oldest confession of faith and its most comprehensive affirmation. It is the central content of the church's "exhibition of the kingdom of heaven to the world." Jesus, this Galilean born in Bethlehem whose life and actions took place in a particular time and place—Palestine in the first century—is the Christ, the Messiah, the anointed One, the one set apart and designated by God for his purposes. And this One is the Lord, "the Word [become] flesh," the One who "was in the beginning with God," the One through whom all things were made, the One who is the bearer of light (John 1:1–4, 14).

In the light of Easter and Pentecost, the Christian community recognized that the kingdom and the king had merged. They looked back upon their experience with Jesus during his earthly ministry, and "their eyes were opened, and they recognized him" (Luke 24:31). All that Jesus had taught and shown about the kingdom of God now began to make astounding new sense: The kingdom had truly "come near" (Mark 1:14) in the incarnation of Jesus and then in the apostolic witness to that event. God's mysterious reign was unveiled in all its glorious and saving purposefulness in the life of Jesus. God disclosed his power, purposefulness, and goodness for all creation and all humanity in Jesus. As we said above, his acts of healing were signs of the kingdom. His teaching was preparation for kingdom obedience. Now it became clear to the emerging church that the Father had truly sent the Son to accomplish God's purposes:

> "For God so loved the world that he gave his only Son, so that everyone who believes in him may not perish but may have eternal life. Indeed, God did not send the Son into the world to condemn the world, but in order that the world might be saved [healed!] through him." (John 3:16–17)

The mysterious character of God's reign is profoundly symbolized in the apparent contradiction of Jesus' death on the cross, his defeat on the world's terms, and the prophetic sign over his head: King of the Jews. As he told Pilate during his trial, "My kingdom is not from this world" (John 18:36). Contrary to all human understandings of the nature and exercise of power, the true king in that chamber was the prisoner Jesus, hands bound and body bleeding. Pilate could not understand that, and the world has never been able to understand the radically different character of the reign of God that has broken in and is drawing near in the lordship of Jesus Christ. This event at the heart of the gospel will always be a scandal and foolishness to many (1 Cor. 1:23).

From Easter onward, however, Christians have been bold to claim that to know this crucified and risen One is to know the heart and the purpose of the Father. To serve this crucified and risen One and to continue his mission is to carry out the will of the Father. The exhibition of the kingdom of heaven to the world is the announcement and practice of the in-breaking reign of God now taking place in the lordship of Jesus Christ.

We have already mentioned Jesus' instruction to pray, "Thy kingdom come, thy will be done, on earth as it is in heaven." And he prepared his disciples to do that will, which was the witness to the kingdom already coming, as he prepared them to become apostles. Mark's Gospel, when describing the calling of the twelve disciples, also makes the important comment "whom he also named apostles"

(Mark 3:14), indicating that the purpose of their discipleship was to be their "sending," that commissioning for apostolic ministry with which each of the Gospels concludes.[3] The Holy Spirit then empowered the apostolic church to recognize in Jesus Christ the very Son of God, God himself revealed within human history. The language that they began to use was truly revolutionary as they witnessed to ". . . the Messiah, who is over all, God blessed forever" (Rom. 9:5). God's reign is revealed and is present in all its power, purposefulness, and goodness in the lordship of Christ. One cannot separate the kingdom of God from the lordship of Christ without diluting the New Testament gospel and falsifying the message and meaning of Jesus' life, death, and resurrection. The kingdom of God is now present in human history in the reign of this Jesus, who is the Christ, the Lord, and the Savior:

> He is the image of the invisible God, the firstborn of all creation; for in him all things in heaven and on earth were created, things visible and invisible, whether thrones or dominions or rulers or powers—all things have been created through him and for him. He himself is before all things, and in him all things hold together. He is the head of the body, the church; he is the beginning, the firstborn from the dead, so that he might come to have first place in everything. For in him all the fullness of God was pleased to dwell, and through him God was pleased to reconcile to himself all things, whether on earth or in heaven, by making peace through the blood of his cross. (Col. 1:15–20)

Out of this confession grows the church's doctrine of the Trinity, the doctrinal exploration of God's self-disclosure as Father, Son, and Holy Spirit. The doctrine became necessary because of the testimony of the early church to what they had encountered. They had encountered God as Father, Son, and Holy Spirit, and therefore they confessed God as the triune God. Trinitarian doctrine is basically the exposition of the lordship of Christ. It follows and interprets the biblical witness, because all the New Testament Scriptures expound the fact and the meaning of the lordship of Jesus Christ—as summarized in the Colossians citation above. It is in following Jesus that the reign of God becomes visible—that is the crux of the sixth Great End, "the exhibition of the kingdom of heaven to the world."

But we remember that Jesus warned his disciples against aping worldly patterns of power. As Jesus made clear in his hearing before Pilate, his reign does not conform to human patterns of authority and monarchy any more than did the God of Israel act like an ancient oriental despot. The power, the purposefulness, and the goodness of God's reign all find ultimate expression in the lordship of Jesus Christ, but it happens in very distinctive ways. Just as the gospel of the cross is folly and stumbling block to contemporaries then and now, the way in which Jesus reigns moves counter to all human patterns of power and authority.

Similarly, the inauguration of the kingdom does not follow human patterns or expectations. We cannot project, or manipulate, or program its inception. We don't possess the blueprints of the kingdom. We don't build it. We are invited into it. We receive it as a gift. We experience it as little children. It comes because God has started it and God will finish it. As Jesus says in the little parable of the growing seed (Mark 4:26ff):

"The kingdom of God is as if someone would scatter seed on the ground, and would sleep and rise night and day, and the seed would sprout and grow, he does not know how. The earth produces of itself, first the stalk, then the head, then the full grain in the head. But when the grain is ripe, at once he goes in with his sickle, because the harvest has come."

To summarize: In Jesus Christ, the kingdom is both here, and is still coming.[4] There is both fulfillment and intensified expectation in the event of Jesus Christ and his reign. God's promise of healing is fulfilled on the cross. The forgiveness of sins and the reconciliation of estranged humanity are accomplished in Jesus' sacrifice. In his victorious resurrection, the power of death over humanity is broken and new life is made possible. It is possible to live now in the certainty that the same resurrection awaits all of us, as we follow Christ: ". . . we know that the one who raised the Lord Jesus will raise us also with Jesus, and will bring us with you into his presence" (2 Cor. 4:14). As Peter puts it in his first letter, the resurrection of Jesus from the dead creates in us a living hope and the confidence in an inheritance that is kept undefiled for us in heaven (1 Pet. 1:3–4).

But this victory, now won, does not yet bring about the end of history and the immediate initiation of a "new heaven and a new earth" (Rev. 21:1). Although the powers that oppose God are already vanquished, the final consummation of all history is still in the future. For a time, we contend with the vestiges of human rebellion that can be very powerful. Jesus himself, as he taught about the in-breaking kingdom, prepared his disciples for the opposition and rejection they would experience as they witnessed to its coming. His own encounter with profound temptation (Matt. 4:1–11; Luke 4:1–13) foreshadowed the seductions that would constantly threaten his followers. But he also promised them that they would not be overcome by the powers and seductions of this world.

Jesus through his Spirit forms his apostolic community to continue its life and work in the full confidence that God "who began a good work among you will bring it to completion by the day of Jesus Christ" (Phil. 1:6). The outcome is already certain—the story will end in the revelation of the ultimate victory of God's love over all opposition. Faith enables us to "set all [our] hope on the grace that Jesus Christ will bring you when he is revealed" (1 Pet. 1:13). That certainty shines like a light out of the future into our lives now and illumines our path. We walk, as subjects of King Jesus, with confidence toward the promised outcome. But the pathway leads through a world that resists its own healing and prefers to follow gods other than the One who is Lord.

We are drawn into that victory when we respond to God's love with faith. We emphasize again: The lordship of Christ, just like the dominion of God the Creator, does not function through coercion, nor through the imposition of God's will. The reign of God becomes our reality when we acknowledge our sin, submit to God's judgment, and receive instead of deserved punishment the gift of cleansing, hope, and new life. At the heart of that newness is the God-given power to confess what God has done, to make known that God's reign has broken in and is now present in Jesus Christ, and to "exhibit" what that looks like. The church is the community of all those who have received this gift of healing together with the desire and ability to pass on this good news. This constitutes the first Great End of the church: "the proclamation of the gospel for the salvation of humankind," which with this last Great End, summarizes and centers the church's understanding of who it is and what it is for.[5]

The kingdom of heaven is then both present and anticipated in the life and witness of Jesus' people. We always live within the realistic tension of what God has already done and what God is most certainly going to do. Secure in that knowledge of God's accomplished action in the past and the confidence of future completion, the Christian community can carry out its calling now. The present is shaped by

God's past and God's future, both of which powerfully illumine and focus our life and action. We live by faith, which is God's gift of the "shield" (Eph. 6:16) that we need for our passage. Peter tells us that God gives us faith as a "guard" to guide us as we await "a salvation ready to be revealed in the last time" (1 Pet. 1:5).

To understand the central claims of the "reign of God" in Christ, we need to emphasize that this is not just a statement that Christians make, perhaps in a liturgy. It is the definition of a new reality. All authority really *has* been given to Jesus in heaven and on earth, and that makes a profound difference in this "now" shaped by the past and the future. Mark's Gospel tells us that when Jesus called the twelve disciples, to initiate their training for apostolate, his purpose was that they should "be with him, and . . . *be* sent out to proclaim the message, and to have authority to cast out demons" (Mark 3:14–15, italics added for emphasis). Here we come to a "second fundamental characteristic of [Jesus'] kingdom ministry: it launches an all-out attack on evil in all its manifestations."[6]

That attack takes place, again, in a way very different from human campaigns. Jesus does not mount a frontal attack on the bastions of evil in the world—he does not counter violence with violence. He turns to the victims of evil and provides them healing, restoration, and newness of life. However the evil manifests itself, be it as sickness, disability, immorality, prejudice, marginalization, or injustice, Jesus touches and heals those so victimized. His kingdom enters into warfare with the rebellious "powers and principalities" as he takes the side of those who suffer, who are cast aside, who are hopeless within a world that rejects both God's goodness and God's purposes. The power of God's reign in Christ is expressed through actions of love and salvation, focused on the "lowly and the despised."

So often, these victims of human evil are, by human standards, helpless in their plight. But the power of God's love is made plain in that they are helped and given new life. For that reason, their physical healing, the forgiveness of their sins, and the redress of the injustice to which they are subjected cannot be separated. The woman caught in adultery is rescued from human injustice when Jesus prevents her stoning, and she is set on a new path of life, cleansed of immorality (John 8:2–11). The paralytic has his sins forgiven and takes up his bed and walks home (Mark 2:1–12). Jesus laid out the agenda of the in-breaking kingdom when he opened the book of Isaiah in the Nazareth synagogue and quoted this text:

"The Spirit of the Lord is upon me,

    because he has anointed me

        to bring good news to the poor.

He has sent me to proclaim release to the captives

    and recovery of sight to the blind,

        to let the oppressed go free,

to proclaim the year of the Lord's favor." (Luke 4:18–19)

This message enraged all those who thought that they had the real power. They almost killed him. Finally, they did. Jesus, in total solidarity with the poor, the captives, the blind, and the oppressed, ends his life as the victim of human wickedness and rebellion against God's goodness. But the most mysterious aspect of God's reign is his sovereign power to transform events that are totally contrary to his goodness into instruments that serve his saving purposes. That is what happened on the cross. Jesus' death was an execution, an act carried out by a government as a political tactic. His death was intended to end a problem for the powers of that day. But this act carried out by rebellious powers and principalities was the event that overturned finally their power and inaugurated the long-expected reign of God. The king whose crown is thorns is the king who *is* the power, and purposefulness, and goodness of God, now ruling over all and bringing about the blessing of the nations. Under his reign, the "year of the Lord's favor" (Luke 4:19) has broken into human history, and it is now the task of the church to exhibit this kingdom of heaven to the world.

The "kingdom of heaven" is then best understood as the biblical way of describing God's word and action in human history, centered upon Jesus Christ.[7] "The kingdom of God is to be interpreted in the light of Jesus Christ."[8] His "kingdom is not from this world" (John 18:36) and yet we are instructed to pray that it might come "on earth as it is in heaven" (Matt. 6:10). God's reign is the ongoing process within history in which God's power, purposefulness, and goodness are accomplishing the healing of the nations. Although the term "king" is taken from human experience, this kingdom is clearly not modeled on human governance or governors. It follows an entirely different order and functions in a way entirely different from that of human forms of domination. It starts at the margins of society by human standards. It works through the most unlikely of agents, and its tactics confound human patterns of power and influence. It is unpredictable and fraught with surprise. It looks toward the future, the outcome of God's action, and emphasizes how that future shapes the present. It is more a corporate than an individual process, although God uses individual persons in its formation. It is engaged not by might or power, but by repentance and conversion. It is God's gift and may be received with the truthfulness of children. It is already present, and is yet to come. It confronts human history in the particular history of Jesus: his incarnation, life, teaching, suffering, death, resurrection, and ascension. It is the treasure beyond all other treasures, to be desired more than anything else.

Notes

1. Lesslie Newbigin, *Sign of the Kingdom* (Grand Rapids: Wm. B. Eerdmans, 1980), p. 18.

2. The name of God in Hebrew was not pronounced by pious Jews out of reverence for its holiness; in its place, other allowed titles for God were used. Christian tradition long read this name as "Jehovah," a literal reading of the consonants of the holy name with the vowels of the alternative term used by faithful Jews. Contemporary scholarship has suggested Yahweh or Jahweh as the probable pronunciation. In many versions of the Bible, the holy name of God in the Old Testament is rendered with the word "Lord" printed in capital letters: "LORD." This Hebrew term, technically called the Tetragrammaton, was rendered "Kyrios" by the Jewish scholars who translated the Old Testament into Greek in the intertestamental period.

3. This comment is lacking in some of the most ancient Gospel manuscripts, so that modern translations can include it or designate it as a textual variant (as, for instance, is the case with the NRSV, where it is footnoted). However, it is clearly an ancient text that underlines the apostolic intent of Jesus' discipling.

4. The themes now addressed are concisely surveyed by David Bosch in *Transforming Mission: Paradigm Shifts in Theology of Mission* (Maryknoll, NY: Orbis Books, 1991), pp. 31–35.

5. Thus we are reiterating the major themes here which have already been explored by Catherine Gunsalus González in her study of the first Great End in this series.

6. Bosch, *Transforming Mission*, p. 32.

7. This summary follows the argument of K. L. Schmidt in his exposition of "BASILEIA" in Gerhard Kittel, ed., *Theologisches Wörterbuch zum Neuen Testament* (Stuttgart, Kohlhammer, 1933), I: 579–592.

8. Howard A. Snyder, *Models of the Kingdom* (Nashville: Abingdon Press, 1991), p. 128.

Questions for Reflection and Discussion

1. How do you react to the claim that Jesus' earthly teaching and preaching centered on the theme of the kingdom of God? How does that claim compare to your ideas about who Jesus was and what he taught?

2. If Christians took seriously Jesus' frequent emphasis that we are to leave harvesting to God, how would our conduct toward nonbelievers and followers of other religions be affected?

3. How is the message of the cross "scandalous" and "foolish" for us today, whether we are Christians or nonbelievers?

4. Some have said that the lordship of Christ is the most compromised and diluted of the Christian faith claims, at least in our Western tradition. How does the central New Testament creed, "Jesus Christ is Lord," challenge the ways we typically think and act as Christians today?

5. Looking back on the discussion of the sixth Great End thus far, what are some of the most significant misconceptions of the "kingdom of God" that you observe in our Christian communities? How does our understanding of the lordship of Christ and the kingdom of God need to change, and what might be the consequences of such changes?

5

Exhibition as Witness: Integrating the Great Ends

What does the sixth Great End of the church mean when it describes the church's task as "exhibition"? How does *exhibition* differ from "the *proclamation* of the gospel for the salvation of humankind," from "the *shelter, nurture,* and *spiritual fellowship* of the children of God," from "the *maintenance* of divine worship," from "the *preservation* of the truth," and from the "*promotion* of social righteousness"? These important nouns do not differ so much as they complement each other. There is obviously much overlap in their meanings. The six Great Ends cannot be properly understood if they are taken in isolation from one another. They present different perspectives on the central focus of the church's calling to be the witness in the world to the good news of God's love in Jesus Christ. They draw out different complementary facets of the church's missional vocation. What precedes and underlies all of them is the basic claim made earlier in Chapter 1 of the Form of Government in the *Book of Order:* "Christ calls the Church into being, giving it all that is necessary for its mission to the world, for its building up, and for its service to God" (G-1.0100b).

To define the distinctive contribution of the term "exhibition" to our total understanding of the church's Great Ends, let us review again what we mean by "church," this movement whose Great Ends we are examining. Based on the biblical testimony, we can begin our definition of the church by describing it as the people of God, called into being by Christ through his Spirit, to continue that particular work for which Abraham and his descendants were called: Through them "all the families of the earth shall be blessed" (Gen. 12:3). The church is the movement set apart by Jesus, the risen Lord, to be his witnesses "in Jerusalem, in all Judea and Samaria, and to the ends of the earth" (Acts 1:8). It is the community called together by Jesus, to be formed and equipped by him as disciples who become apostles (Mark 3:14), to be the "salt of the earth" and the "light of the world" (Matt. 5:13–16). It is the community to whom Jesus announces at Easter, "As the Father has sent me, so I send you" (John 20:21). It is the movement that emerges from its encounter with the Holy Spirit in the Upper Room of Acts 1 to the open square in Jerusalem of Acts 2 where everyone hears the gospel in his or her own language, and Peter preaches the message on behalf of this newly empowered community. The church is the growing network of communities described in the New Testament, founded by the apostolic witness, each congregation existing to continue the witness that started it. Wherever this called and sent community exists, it is to serve as Christ's letter to the world (see 2 Cor. 3:1–3). It is to be a "spiritual house" and a "holy priesthood, to offer spiritual sacrifices acceptable to God through Jesus Christ" (1 Pet. 2:5). In perhaps the most comprehensive biblical statement of the church's purpose, linking it to the whole sweep of God's history of salvation, Peter states, "You are a chosen race, a royal priesthood, a holy nation, God's own people, in order that you may proclaim the mighty acts of him who called you out of darkness into his marvelous light" (1 Pet. 2:9).

The six Great Ends of the church seek to capture and convey this missional calling of the church as they evoke the essential dimensions of her task described by these ends. The particular thrust of the sixth Great End is the combination of the message of the kingdom of heaven with the assertion that it is to be exhibited to all the world. One could paraphrase it this way: The message that Jesus Christ is the present and coming Lord is to be witnessed to in every aspect of the church's life before and for the sake of the world, as we wait for God to complete the work of reconciliation and healing that God has initiated on the cross and at Easter. Thus, in biblical terms, "exhibition" may be most appropriately interpreted as "witness."[1] It emphasizes "demonstration," "giving evidence," rendering audible and visible the message of the gospel and its meaning in and for the world. The sixth of the Great Ends summarizes all of them missionally by centering everything around the church's calling to be and do concrete witness to the gospel in the world. It integrates the accents of all six Great Ends for "the exhibition of the kingdom of heaven to the world." It is about the church's task to make known what is fundamentally knowable since Easter and Pentecost. It is about demonstrating that the kingdom of heaven is breaking in now wherever the lordship of Jesus Christ is confessed and practiced. It is about God's love for all the world, which results in God's sending the witnessing community "to the ends of the earth." To "exhibit the kingdom of heaven to the world" is to be, to do, and to carry out Spirit-empowered witness to the in-breaking reign of God personified by Jesus Christ, the rising and now reigning Lord. Understanding "exhibition" as "witness" reveals how powerfully the sixth Great End integrates and summarizes the preceding five.

"Exhibition" necessarily relates to the central purpose of the church, the "proclamation of the gospel for the salvation of humankind." This first Great End focuses on the verbal communication of the good news. The mission of the church in all its dimensions is defined by and relates to this purpose: Proclaim the gospel. By linking proclamation and exhibition, we challenge the pernicious tendency to separate word from act, which is a besetting sin of Western Christendom. The gospel is "the power of God for salvation" (Rom. 1:16). Like the Word of God that creates in Genesis 1 ("And God said, let there be . . ."), the announcement of the gospel is the event of good news happening. Thus, the spoken witness and the demonstrated witness cannot be separated, if one is faithful to the New Testament.

For this reason, Jesus tells the disciples immediately prior to his ascension that they will be "be my witnesses"—their very existence is defined by the calling to be witness. This linkage is also emphasized constantly in the New Testament by the transitions from indicative statements (describing the event of the gospel) to imperative statements (drawing out the concrete implications of the gospel). Proclamation or communication of the good news is the essential and defining center of the church's calling, but its mission is only adequately defined when that verbal center is surrounded by the demonstration of the in-breaking reign in every dimension of the church's life "before a watching world" (to borrow a phrase from John Howard Yoder). This essential linkage is emphasized then by the subsequent Great Ends.

The most important visible form of Christian witness is the living out of its gospel calling by the witnessing community. The formation of that corporate witness is an overarching concern of the New Testament Scriptures. As we have emphasized above, God calls and sets apart a particular people to be the instrument of his healing purposes for the world. If the "children of God" are to be faithful to their calling, then their "shelter, nurture, and spiritual fellowship" are crucial.

By stressing the church's calling as witness to the world, the sixth Great End emphasizes that the church's "shelter, nurture, and spiritual fellowship" are not isolated ends in themselves. The point of the church's calling is not merely that the church should exist, be sheltered and nurtured, and enjoy its spiritual fellowship. Of course, Christendom reveals many ways in which Western Christians have understood the "shelter, nurture, and spiritual fellowship of the children of God" as an end in itself. Then the church, as an institution, tends to exist for itself and its members. It concentrates inwardly on its members' needs and desires. It can become preoccupied with its status as the community of the saved. It may attempt to decide who is saved and who is not. Often the church has equated "savedness" with church membership! If the "spiritual fellowship of the children of God" loses sight of its calling to "proclaim the gospel for the salvation of humankind," or of its mandate to "exhibit the kingdom of heaven to the world," the danger is real that it will become a spiritual club of the like-minded, incapable of faithful witness to the world. This is the classic image of the church as a kind of Dead Sea into which the river of revelation and faith flows while nothing flows out.

The first and sixth Great Ends, bracketing the entire definition, emphasize that the church is called to be a divinely ordained means to God's end for the world. Thinking about the church in this way shifts our focus away from the church in two directions: to God's self-disclosure in Jesus Christ, who is the one in whom God's reign is breaking in, and to the world for whose healing Jesus was sent. The wording of the sixth Great End can be a corrective to possible distortions of the church's calling—there is more than enough evidence of such distortion in the long history of the church!

Divine worship is the focal point of the "exhibition" of the kingdom of heaven, for here public witness is made to the presence and lordship of Christ. Here, in word, sacrament, prayer, and praise, the community of faith not only "exhibits" the lordship of Christ but is equipped to be sent out to witness to it. The church must "maintain divine worship" if it is going to be able to respond to its calling and be Christ's letter to the world. In its gathered life, the community of witnesses is being "written" as "a letter of Christ" (2 Cor. 3:1–3) so that it can be sent (*mission* means "sending"!) out into the world. In Mark's account of the calling of the Twelve, to which we have already referred (Mark 3:13ff), the evangelist emphasizes that their calling was first of all to be with Jesus before they were sent out to proclaim his message. Both the "shelter, nurture, and spiritual fellowship of the children of God" and the "maintenance of divine worship" are the concrete ways in which we live with Jesus in our midst in order to be sent out by him.

But, again, one can "maintain divine worship" in ways that fail to "exhibit the kingdom of heaven to the world." The worship practices of the church, if they become an end in themselves, can degenerate into empty ritual or aesthetic performance. Rather than being the "work of the people," the liturgy can become a vehicle for clergy to function as spiritual performers providing religious experiences for the audience of worshipers. The music of worship will then often be little more than a concert; and the beauty of worship, intended to praise and extol the greatness and glory of God, will serve instead to spotlight the aesthetic sensibilities and talents of humanity. The architecture that provides spaces for divine worship can become an object of its own idolatry, and the arts and crafts that should and can serve to enrich genuine worship can become alternative objects of worship.

In modern societies, like ours, pervasively shaped by individualism and consumerism, "divine worship" can degenerate into "programs that meet the religious needs of their attenders." We borrow from the perspectives of popular psychology, entertainment culture, consumer research, and therapy, to transform "divine worship" into choreographed events that focus on making us feel good. Christendom's ancient pattern of partnership between church and state is often replaced today by a partnership between church and marketplace. And in that partnership, the religious marketplace defines what is "successful." Thus, in a myriad of ways the "maintenance" of divine worship can become a hindrance to the mission of the church.

Without the "preservation of the truth" there is no "exhibition of the kingdom of heaven to the world"! Everything centers on the distinctive message of God's once-and-for-all intervention in human history through the event of Jesus Christ, and what it means. The church preserves the truth by its constant exploration of what this event has meant, now means, and will ultimately mean. That exploration is the missional task of theological work, and it is essential for the church's faithful obedience to its calling. Our own healing is dependent on our being "transformed by the renewing of our minds" (Rom. 12:2), and the "preservation of the truth" serves that process. This is not a static process, a mere repetition of what others have said, but a claiming and converting process, in which the truth of Christ constantly challenges and changes us.

What happens, then, when the "preservation of the truth" is severed from the calling to missional witness? If the preservation of the truth is not inextricably linked with the exhibition of the kingdom of heaven to the world, then we can turn doctrine into an idol. If the truth we are preserving is abstracted from the purpose of that truth, which is God's saving love for the world, then it becomes falsehood. The truth that God reveals, to which the Bible witnesses, is always personal—that is, it is always related to the loving and self-disclosing God whom we know as Father through the Son whom he sent. To preserve the truth is to practice faithfulness to the great tradition of faith that links the New Testament community through all the intervening generations to the church around the world today. When the church is committed to the exhibition of the kingdom of heaven to the world, then it preserves the truth in order to witness to it, to point toward the one who is the way, the truth, and the life. This understanding of the importance of the way in which the truth is preserved profoundly shapes how the exhibition of the kingdom of heaven should take place. We will return to this theme in the next chapter.

"The promotion of social righteousness" may be the most obvious and most readily agreed upon aspect of the church's calling. Yet, even the promotion of social righteousness can, if separated from the exhibition of the kingdom of heaven to the world, be distorted. The social witness of the church has to do with the implications of the gospel for every dimension of public and private life. It has to do with the confrontation of human sin and rebellion, because of the healing of forgiveness; it moves toward the transformation of that sin into a radically new way of living within the world that demonstrates the goodness of God's rule. To promote social righteousness is, then, to exhibit the concrete shape of the lordship of Christ.

We often observe what happens to the commitment to the promotion of social righteousness when it is divorced from the other Great Ends, and especially from the "exhibition of the kingdom of heaven to the world." That divorce is at work when we hear language about the kingdom of God using verbs we don't find in the New Testament: We are building the kingdom; we are introducing the kingdom; we are strategizing the kingdom. God's mysterious reign has become our program of social justice, to be implemented by us (perhaps with God's help). In isolation from the other five Great Ends, the fifth can become an ideology, a political program emerging from a particular social and historical context, and thus an arrogant assumption that the kingdom is under our control and at our disposal.

There are many dimensions of "witness," as expounded in Scripture, which help, then, to unpack what "exhibition of the kingdom of heaven to the world" means. We have begun to explore this question by affirming that this exhibition is best understood as the "witness" about which we read so much in the New Testament, especially in Acts. "Witness" is a comprehensive term in the New

Testament that relates every aspect of the church's life and action to its calling. Several words in New Testament Greek are based on the root for "witness"—the term from which we derive the word "martyr" in English. One form of the word defines the individual believer as a witness. This is the form used by Jesus when he announces the purpose of the church in Acts 1:8: "You will be my witnesses." Another form of the word refers to the impact made on the world because the witnessing community is present. That "exhibition of the kingdom of heaven" is the outworking of the witnessing community's presence and action as light, leaven, and salt. It is what happens because the missional community is fundamentally public—it is meant to be seen, and heard, and reacted to. This calling as witness, as we have argued in the previous chapter, is comprehensive: It relates to everything we are, we do, and we say.

The biblical understanding of "witness," going back to the Old Testament, is rooted in the practices of courts of law. The role of the witness in legal procedure is to give evidence so that others may make important decisions: Juries and judges come to their findings based on the evidence provided by witnesses. This is the sense in which the Bible uses the concept of "witness." Witnesses point away from themselves to what has happened, and to what that happening might mean. Witnesses don't pass judgment; they don't determine who is saved and who is lost. The witness does not move from that seat to the judge's bench in order to pass sentence. The promise of the Spirit to the church is that our all too human efforts as witnesses can and will be used by God to foster the in-breaking of God's good reign in Christ and to further the healing of the nations. This exhibition of the kingdom of heaven, then, will truly communicate with the whole world for which it is intended if the church pays close attention to the way in which Scripture lays out the task of witness and how it is to be done.

The crucial biblical question, as far as the witness is concerned, is its authenticity, reliability, and trustworthiness. Everything depends on witnesses who tell the truth and give credible testimony. Thus, there is great emphasis in the New Testament, first of all, on the integrity of the church's witness. Especially in the Pauline letters we find a continuing concern for the truthfulness and sincerity of Christian witness. What is exhibited to the world needs to be, in every way, a demonstration of the powerfulness, purposefulness, and goodness of the kingdom of heaven. In the earliest writing in the New Testament, 1 Thessalonians, we encounter the apostle's exposition of witnessing integrity:

For our appeal does not spring from deceit or impure motives or trickery, but just as we have been approved by God to be entrusted with the message of the gospel, even so we speak, not to please mortals, but to please God who tests our hearts. As you know and as God is our witness, we never came with words of flattery or with a pretext for greed; nor did we seek praise from mortals, whether from you or from others. (1 Thess. 2:3–6)

There are obvious temptations to distort the gospel, which have been present and at work ever since Jesus contended with Satan's temptations in the wilderness. This greatest of all truth, the story of God's love, can be dealt with deceitfully, and it can be co-opted by "impure motives" and "trickery." There are more than enough sad examples of that degrading of the gospel in today's "electronic church." It would be hypocritical for us to point at other traditions with such accusations and not face the problems of integrity within our own denominational family. Are we not also constantly tempted to reshape the gospel so that it will "please mortals," or "fit well into our cultural context," or "align with the dominant thought patterns of our society," or, more mundanely, "please the big givers"? Are there no traces of self-interest in our divisions? Are there not questionable forms of game playing and power brokering in our governance? Within every organized form of the church, there is plenty of evidence of mortals who use the gospel to build their own egos and fortunes.

All of this serves as a warning, going back to the very earliest days of the church, that the exhibition of the kingdom of heaven to the world must be characterized by faithfulness both to the message and to the methods of Jesus. If we understand the exhibition of the kingdom of heaven as the witness to the lordship of Jesus Christ, then that witness begins with the earthly ministry of Jesus. There is where we learn what that integrity looks like. We will explore this theme in greater detail in the next chapter.

Second, the biblical witness that carries out this task of "exhibition" is corporate by definition. It is the witness of the entire community, the witness for which the entire community is called into existence by God's Spirit. At Pentecost, the community is born with the task to "be Christ's witness." From the selection of the Twelve on, the New Testament constantly emphasizes that Jesus' purpose was to find and form a community to continue in the calling originally given to Abraham for Israel. The choice of twelve persons calls to mind "the people of God." This community is, of course, made up of individuals each of whom is personally called by Christ into his service. They are all people whom Christ desired as his followers (see Mark 3:13). But once called, they are now molded and formed by him into a community of witness, living with him and learning from him in order to be sent out by him. They are instructed, in a great range of ways, that their life together is their first form of witness: "By this everyone will know that you are my disciples, if you have love for one another" (John 13:35).

The love that God has for the world and which causes him to send his Son now becomes the primary characteristic of the community that the Son is sending into the world. "Witness" refers to every dimension of the community's life, not just to its oral testimony. That is why Jesus tells the disciples on the Mount of the Ascension that they will *be* his witnesses—which is far more comprehensive than if he had said, "You shall give testimonies." What he intends is a community that is a continuing exhibition of the in-breaking kingdom of heaven, an ongoing demonstration of the gracious and healing rule of King Jesus.

Third, the witnessing community knows that it is called and sent, wherever it is. It has a clear sense of its mission. At various places in the New Testament, this community is called "ecclesia," which we translate as "church." In the Greek world from which that term was taken, it referred to a public assembly, a group of people meeting and acting with a commission to do public business. The basic idea of the word is an assembly that is called and set apart to do public business. To speak of its "calling" is to emphasize that this community is the result of someone else's action. It does not call itself into existence, but rather it comes to life because God has already acted. Jesus forms the community of the disciples by calling each one to join him. None of them applied to become a disciple. He "desired" each one, and they were obedient to that call. Then, they gradually learned the purpose of their calling, which was to be the witness to the world of what they had encountered in their life with Jesus. The whole story, from their initial calling to their commissioning at Easter and Pentecost, becomes the content of their witness. This entire understanding of the church as fundamentally missional underlies the choice of the term "ecclesia"—a public assembly to carry out tasks that are important for everyone.

"We declare to you what was from the beginning, what we have heard, what we have seen with our eyes, what we have looked at and touched with our hands, concerning the word of life . . . what we have seen and heard so that you also may have fellowship with us . . . ."

(1 John 1:1–3). The witnesses, joined together in a newly empowered community, give evidence to the world about what they have encountered as they responded to God calling them to be followers of Jesus. That calling has made them into a community with a distinctive purpose, an "ecclesia." That purpose is witness, which is exhibition and demonstration before the world of the fact of the lordship of Christ and the meaning of the lordship of Christ.

Note

1. The most comprehensive treatment of Christian calling as witness is found in Karl Barth, *Church Dogmatics*, trans. G. W. Bromiley (Edinburgh: T. & T. Clark, 1961, IV,2,2, second half, in his discussion of "The Vocation of Man," pp. 481–680. The crux of the argument is in "The Christian as Witness," pp. 554–613. My own modest exploration of this theme is documented in the volumes cited in note 15.

Questions for Reflection and Discussion

1. Guder defines *exhibition* as "witness." Do you agree with this definition? What other verbs might be used to expound the meaning of *exhibition?*

2. How does the understanding of "witness" expounded in this chapter differ from other ways that Christians use this term?

3. How would one critique the idea that a church should "meet the religious needs of its members," based on the understanding of the church's calling developed in this chapter (and in the previous Great Ends)?

4. How is the biblical concern for the "integrity" of the community's witness relevant to church reality today?

5. In this chapter, there are several examples of the problems that result when the six Great Ends are not understood as mutually complementary and defining. What are some other possible consequences of emphasizing one or the other Great End at the expense of their collective meaning?

Exhibition as Incarnational Witness: The Struggle for Congruence[1]

6

What does the exhibition of the kingdom of heaven actually look like? How do all six Great Ends coalesce in the actual conduct of the worshiping and witnessing congregation? In this chapter, we will propose that the incarnation of Jesus Christ defines the way that congregations are formed for "the exhibition of the kingdom of heaven to the world." To do this, however, we will have to revisit some aspects of the Christendom legacy that we discussed in Chapter 1.

We have linked exhibition as witness to the central claim that the kingdom of heaven is present and knowable through the lordship of Jesus Christ. We have also stated that the formation of that witness takes place today as it took place with the first Christians: in the formation that Jesus himself carries out with his followers. This aspect of formation for exhibition of the kingdom of heaven needs now to be explored further.

To be a disciple of Jesus is to engage in a process of learning and equipping that results in apostolate. To come to Jesus means that one is sent out by Jesus. This is the pattern established in Mark's description of the calling of the Twelve "to be with him, and to be sent out to proclaim the message" (Mark 3:14). Thus, the exhibition of the kingdom of heaven to the world can only happen as the called community is formed for that witness by its encounter with Jesus, the first-century rabbi who ministered in Palestine in the first century. The "how" of exhibition is addressed by the disciples' formation depicted in the four Gospels, and reflected by the apostles as they continued the formation of their churches in their epistles. To put it another way, the incarnation of God's Son in Jesus Christ is both the central event of the gospel, and, at the same time, it defines how this event is to be made known. The witness to the gospel is both its message and the way that it is communicated. As we said above, there is a profound concern in the New Testament for the integrity of the witness of Christian communities. Given the enormous distortions we inherit in the understanding of "kingdom," "rule," "lordship," and "power," our starting question is an urgent and challenging one: What does the *exhibition of the kingdom of heaven to the world* actually look like? To put it another way: How does the message of the incarnation become incarnational in the being, doing, and saying of Christian congregations? The way that we deal with this difficult question will have an impact on the realization of all six Great Ends of the Church in our congregations. And it is in these congregations, shaped by the legacy of Christendom, that we encounter both the potential for our faithful response to the Great Ends of the Church, and the many forms of resistance to the corporate conversion that such faithfulness requires.

This question of "incarnational faithfulness" has become urgent as Christendom gradually comes to an end in the Western world. As part of the Christendom legacy, Presbyterians have to confront the fact that the "exhibition of the kingdom of heaven to the world" does not happen, for us, in a vacuum. We have to deal straightforwardly with the many ways in which the Western Christian tradition has diluted, compromised, and reduced both the gospel and the church's mandate over the centuries. We can only discover how, with integrity, we should exhibit the kingdom of heaven to the world, as we honestly address the history that has often jeopardized that integrity.

One of the symptoms of the gradual disintegration of Western Christendom has been, for at least a century, the gnawing sense that the legacy was in trouble. This became obvious toward the end of the twentieth century as the religious statistics of North Atlantic societies revealed enormous losses in members and commitment. But the problems were surfacing in a variety of ways long before the issue of membership loss became a public theme. Without claiming to be comprehensive, we can look at several ways in which Western Christianity has struggled with a growing sense of self-questioning.

One of the ways in which Christendom has questioned itself has been the recurring call for the renewal of the church. Like the prophets calling the ancient kings of Israel into question, there have been voices and movements that challenged the church with some version of this question: Are we the church that Jesus intended? Are we following the patterns of Jesus' ministry as we continue his mission? The monastic movement, in its many waves and expressions, constantly challenged the institutional church in Europe with a vision of a more faithful and more authentic discipleship. St. Francis may serve as one example of such a call to restored faithfulness, but there are countless others before and after him. The Reformation of the sixteenth century was an appeal for the cleansing of the church, for a reclamation of its evangelical purpose and integrity.[2] Both Luther and Calvin, and later Wesley, were profoundly concerned about the integrity of the life of the Christian church. For them, conduct and doctrine were inextricably linked. As we move into the modern period, we continue to see such appeals for reformation and renewal, especially in the various revivals and awakenings that occurred in the eighteenth and nineteenth centuries.

Such appeals were not without good cause. No one can deny the constant slippage of the Christian movement into patterns of compromise and gospel reductionism that, at times, were a virtual betrayal of the gospel and the church's mission. In the first chapter, we spoke about the problems we have understanding the concept of "king" and "kingdom" after centuries of compromise with human patterns of power and violence in Western Christendom. We are keenly aware of the many forms of corruption within the institutional church evidenced in its history, of the ways that power, wealth, and lust have taken control of its leadership, of profound distortions of its calling like the Crusades, the Inquisition, the execution of heretics, and doctrinal justifications of violence and cruelty.

The intellectual Enlightenment of the seventeenth and eighteenth centuries was in many ways a reaction to the devastation of the wars of religion that scarred Europe in the century after the Reformation. That violence, most of it centered on the question of Christian identity (would European principalities be Catholic, Lutheran, Reformed, or something else?), made it difficult to proclaim Jesus Christ as Prince of peace! European thinkers rejected much of traditional Christianity precisely because it appeared to them to foster such inhumanity, and they opted for human reason as a more reliable way than religion to bring about virtuous conduct. It has been said that Marx should be understood as a reaction to the failure of European Christendom to live out the message of Jesus. What he was trying to do, one might say, was to implement the kingdom of God, as envisioned in Jesus' teaching (especially the Sermon on the Mount), but without God, who had become an enormous problem if not a disappointment. Gandhi frequently spoke of his high esteem of Jesus and his teaching, but found that Western Christianity did not fulfill that vision. David Bosch commented at one point that the history of Western theology could be described as a sequence of learned attempts to explain why the Sermon on the Mount did not apply to us![3] Although tongue in cheek, there is certainly merit to what he says!

The final blow for Western Christendom has been the catastrophic wars of the twentieth century, both of which were unleashed by so-called Christian countries against other so-called Christian countries. The German kaiser's declaration of war against England and France in 1914 was supported by an impressive list of German Protestant theologians, whose public statement endorsing the war drove Karl Barth back to his Bible, to Romans, and to the confrontational gospel of sin and redemption. The world had never experienced such total war as was unleashed by the nations of Western Christendom against each other. It is still difficult to comprehend the inhumanities of the Third Reich, especially its programmatic extermination of the Jews. The irony is that all of the Western European armies (except the Soviet Russians) engaged in those wars had Christian chaplains ministering to their troops! Christendom had clearly degenerated to such a point that the consensus was already being articulated in the 1930s that Western Christianity was in obvious decline.

This process of decline in the West was paralleled by the rapid expansion of Christianity into a global movement beyond the boundaries of Western Christendom. This was the consequence of the foreign mission movement of the eighteenth to the twentieth centuries. By the middle of the twentieth century, it was clear that European Christianity was only one part of the worldwide Christian movement, and that it was, in fact, a diminishing part. The growth of the Christian church has moved from the global north to the global south.[4]

From its inception, of course, the Western mission movement was also weighted with its own ambiguities. It was profoundly influenced by Western "Enlightened" thinking that assumed that European cultures represented the highest achievement of human civilization. The Christian missionaries who spread across the globe were inspired by a vision to "bring to the world the benefits of the gospel and of western civilization."[5] The importance of their undoubted commitment to Christ and willingness to give their lives for his gospel cannot be diminished. But we must recognize that they were largely reading the world through Western Christendom glasses, reflecting the sense of cultural superiority that conditioned anyone born into Western cultures.

In spite of that fact, the missionaries' encounter with the non-Christian world beyond the boundaries of Western Christendom had an enormous impact not only upon those they evangelized but upon the westerners as well. Their movement out of the safety and security of Christendom became a movement of discovery about the problems of Christendom that were largely unrecognized within its boundaries. Now they were outside those boundaries. The safety and security were not there. Whereas in Europe they were part of an established so-called Christian culture, and thus lived with the comfortable sense of being in the majority, in the mission fields they were part of a very small minority. Even as they assumed that their mission was to bring the Western church and culture as necessary partners of the gospel, that assumption began to falter. As they put the gospel into more and more languages (often rendering these oral languages into written ones in the process), they themselves began to recognize the problems of the Christendom legacy that had shaped them. They began to wonder whether it was really possible to equate European Christianity with the Christian movement centered upon Jesus Christ. Could Christendom continue to assume that it represented, in fact, normative Christianity for the whole world?

These questions opened up as a whole range of issues came to the fore in the newly emerging non-Western churches. Perhaps the most obvious problem were the divisions of European Christendom that the Western missionaries exported to the newly emerging churches. Within the boundaries of Christendom, we had long since made our peace with our divisions, and had even learned theologically to justify them. But in the minority situation of the mission field, Western missionaries soon realized that their dividedness was an obstacle to evangelization and ultimately a betrayal of the gospel they were proclaiming. When they were expounding Jesus' message of the kingdom of God in non-Western contexts, European Christendom's dilutions and distortions of this basic message began to emerge in high relief. The Christian communities emerging in those contexts began to realize that there was a very great difference between the Jesus of the biblical testimonies, and the religiosity that their missionaries had brought them. They were especially concerned about the divisions among Christians that were part of the modern missionary movement. In a remarkable way, these Christian brothers and sisters continued to appreciate the labors of their missionaries while at the same time sorting out the accretions of Christendom that were part of the missionaries' heritage. That process is still going on—we discuss it today as the task of ongoing contextualization.

Looking back, one can say that the concern for the unity of the church which emerged out of the nineteenth-century mission fields, and which generated the modern ecumenical movement, was at its core a concern for the integrity of the gospel in the emerging churches of the non-Western world. The missionaries were not incarnating the radical gospel of Christ if their message included a judgment or even a dismissal of Christian brothers and sisters from another European tradition, actively proclaiming just down the road in the next village. This was often more obvious to the emerging churches than it was to the sending churches!

The issue of church division was only one of the ways in which the disjunction between message and communication became obvious when missionaries moved across the cultural borders of Christendom. The relationship between colonialism and the missionary movement was often a glaring example of the problem. Those ancient patterns of church–state partnership were replicated when missionaries served as agents of colonial control. That was not always happening, of course. Over and over again, missionaries resisted the attempts at commercial exploitation and political repression of the indigenous peoples, which were the common strategies of the colonizing agencies. In some regions, the missionary presence was such a problem for colonizing agencies that their governments banned the missionaries! For the governments of Christendom, profit and power often were ultimately more important than proclaiming the "truth of the gospel." But, inevitably, Western Christendom's confusion about the relationship of the kingdom of God to human kingdoms became a factor in the formation of new Christian communities on the mission field.

As missionaries told the story of Jesus in non-European tongues and accompanied converts in the formation of churches that were shaped by the biblical witness, their sensitivity to Christendom's compromises and cultural captivity grew. They were confronted with the problem of missional integrity in a great diversity of ways. It is no exaggeration to say that the Western missionaries experienced their own ongoing conversion as they participated in Christian mission beyond the safe boundaries of Christendom. They were being helped to see the gospel without the centuries-old lenses of Western social compromise. In the crucible of cross-cultural engagement, many of their unquestioned assumptions were placed in question. Structures that were unquestioned came under scrutiny. This was reflected in diverse ways. Women assumed positions of leadership on the mission field that were completely inaccessible to them in their home churches. Social class and background often meant much less on the mission field than they did back in Europe. William Carey was a shoemaker who became, in India, a highly respected scholar of language and culture. The assumed superiority of European cultural forms and intellectual traditions was increasingly questioned.

This process should not be romanticized. Western missionaries continued to struggle with racism and classism well into the twentieth century. They often hindered the genuine indigenization of the gospel through their insistence on Western ways of doing things. There was considerable debate over these issues, and not a little controversy. Some missionaries were ordered home by their sponsoring boards because they had "gone native." That meant that they had moved too far from the European cultural shape of Christian practice and allowed the new Christians too much freedom to become church in ways that authentically worked in their cultures. But, in all that give and take, there was clearly a growing awareness on the part of many that the deeply rooted problems of Western Christendom became much more visible in the changed context of non-European cultures. It was a process that would take decades, but the concern for the integrity of Christian witness gradually filtered back to the sending societies and churches, raising questions about the faithfulness of Western churches in their own cultural context: How were they, in fact, serving as an exhibition of the kingdom of heaven to the world?

In 1928, the Scottish Presbyterian missionary to Peru, John Mackay, wrote a paper on the church's evangelistic mission, in connection with the Jerusalem meeting of the International Missionary Council. By that time, he had become a thoroughly bi-cultural missionary, an expert on the Spanish philosopher Unamuno, and a respected university professor in Peru. Although no less committed to mission and evangelism than he had ever been, he raised concerns about the way in which Western mission had been conducted over the previous decades. He insisted that the way the gospel was communicated was integral to its message. He spoke tellingly of the need to "earn the right to be heard."[6]

Mackay was basically arguing for the essential congruence of missional message and method. Proceeding from the "centrality of Christ" as the foundational premise of the Christian mission, he expounds the "riches of Christ," beginning with a discussion of Christ as the "perfect pattern." This brief exploration of the significance of the humanity and earthly ministry of Christ for his mission is then rooted in a profound emphasis on Jesus Christ as the "incarnate revelation of God." It is a Christology that takes the humanity of Christ seriously without diminishing the Trinitarian confession of the deity of Christ. And it is on the basis of such a Christology that Mackay then investigates "how [to] present the Christian message." The growing missiological preoccupation with the "incarnational" integrity of kingdom exhibition in the twentieth century finds perhaps its earliest articulation here.

If the kingdom of God shapes every dimension of creation and of human life, then its exhibition should show how the lordship of Christ enables his witnesses to point toward that rule in their conduct, their values, their life together, and their teaching. As I have noted, that congruence had often been absent or very weak on the mission field, which led many in the twentieth century to become critics of the Western mission endeavor and even to call for its end. It cast a revealing spotlight on the pervasive incongruence of Western Christianity, which was (and is) made even more objectionable by the way Western churches are both complacent about and even defend their cultural compromises and captivity.

This focus on the congruence of Christian witness in diverse cultures gradually became a consensus in the global discussion of mission. When the World Council's Conference on Mission and Evangelization met in San Antonio in 1989, it concentrated its energies on the theme "Your Will Be Done: Mission in Christ's Way."[7] It was now clear that the kingdom of God could only be exhibited to the world by Christian communities that proclaimed Jesus' message in the way that Jesus did it. This understanding of the distinctive character of Christian witness has repeatedly been interpreted as "incarnational." The Presbyterian Church (U.S.A.) validated this missional principle when it adopted the statement "Turn to the Living God: A Call to Evangelism in Christ's Way" in 1991.[8]

The basic theological conviction expressed by the concept "incarnational witness" is this: *The event of the Gospel constitutes the content of its proclamation and establishes the method of its communication.* This is how the exhibition of the kingdom of heaven to the world fundamentally and centrally takes place. What is exhibited is the truth to which all Scriptures testify, and which we discussed in the first chapters of this book: God's radical and comprehensive love for all creation takes human form in the person and work of Jesus Christ. This event is the history that constitutes the "clue" to human history, what Lesslie Newbigin calls the "open secret."[9] It is the turning point in human history, the movement to a new covenant, a new creation, a new birth, a new reality, and thus a new hope.

As we have argued above, the incarnation of Jesus Christ, as reported in the New Testament Scriptures, is a once-and-for-all event whose validity embraces all the world and all its inhabitants. For that reason, it now may and must be exhibited to the world. This is how we must understand the emphasis in the sixth Great End of the church on the exhibition of the kingdom of heaven *to the world*. For that to happen, God continues the strategy of calling, setting apart, equipping, and sending a people whose purpose is to be a witness to his salvation.

That divine vocational strategy is made clear in the New Testament. Jesus calls the disciples whom he then equips to become apostles. The earthly ministry of Jesus is essential to the Gospel both as disclosure of the message of the kingdom and formation of the disciples to become its witnesses. This understanding of the way in which the gospel event unfolds shapes how we read and interpret the Scriptures, especially the four Gospels. The salvation events of Good Friday and Easter form the climax of each Gospel account. But the story does not start with Holy Week in any of the four versions. It starts with the onset of Jesus' earthly ministry—preceded in two Gospels by nativity and childhood stories. And it reaches its necessary conclusion at Pentecost, when the apostolic community is empowered to become witness throughout the world. For the early Christian communities for which the Gospels were written, the earthly ministry of Jesus was essential formation. They could not become apostles of the risen and ascended Lord if they had not "gone to school" with him, that is, joined the disciples in their intense preparation for the mission that awaited them. In that process of schooling, they learned through the message and the model of Jesus what congruent witness would look like. The once-and-for-all nature of the incarnation is in no way diminished by the insistence that Jesus shows us how the event of in-breaking and saving reign of God is to be transmitted, as it is happening in and through him. The incarnation requires that its message be made known incarnationally, that it be congruent.[10]

So, again, we ask the question What does the exhibition of the kingdom actually look like? How does this witness take shape and become concrete? How is this message of the incarnation communicated to the world incarnationally? How does the church exhibit the kingdom of heaven to the world in ways that are congruent with the character and purpose of that kingdom? We consider these questions in the next and concluding chapter.

Notes

1. Much of the argument in this chapter summarizes my discussion of incarnational witness in *Be My Witnesses: The Church's Mission, Message, and Messengers* (Grand Rapids: Wm. B. Eerdmans, 1985); see also my book *The Incarnation and the Church's Witness* (Harrisburg, PA: Trinity Press International, 1999), re-issued: Salem: Wipf & Stock, 2005.

2. Scott H. Hendrix, *Recultivating the Vineyard: The Reformation Agendas of Christianization* (Louisville: Westminster John Knox Press, 2004).

3. "Through the ages, however, Christians have usually found ways around the clear meaning of the Sermon on the Mount." David Bosch, *Transforming Mission: Paradigm Shifts in Theology of Mission* (Maryknoll, NY: Orbis Books, 1991), p. 69.

4. See Philip Jenkins, *The Next Christendom: The Coming of Global Christianity* (New York: Oxford University Press, 2002).

5. See David Bosch's magisterial exposition of "Mission in the Wake of the Enlightenment," *Transforming Mission*, pp. 262–345.

6. John Mackay, "The Evangelistic Duty of Christianity," in *The Jerusalem Meeting of the International Missionary Council, March 24–April 8, 1928*, vol. I (New York & London: International Missionary Council, 1928), pp. 393f.; the following paragraph summarizes the argument of this essay, pp. 383–397. See also Darrell Guder, "Incarnational Witness and the Church's Evangelistic Mission," *International Review of Mission*, vol. lxxxiii, no. 330, pp. 417–428.

7. Lesslie Newbigin guided the conference into this theme with the Bible Study book that he wrote as its preparatory volume: *Mission in Christ's Way: A Gift, a Command, an Assurance* (New York: Friendship Press), 1987.

8. "Turn to the Living God: A Call to Evangelism in Christ's Way," in *Selected Theological Statements of the Presbyterian Church (U.S.A.) General Assemblies (1956–1998)* [Louisville: Office of Theology and Worship, Presbyterian Church (U.S.A.), 1998], pp. 617–634.

9. Lesslie Newbigin, *The Open Secret: An Introduction to the Theology of Mission*, rev. ed. (Grand Rapids: Wm. B. Eerdmans, 1995).

10. See Darrell Guder, *The Incarnation and the Church's Witness.*

Questions for Reflection and Discussion

1. How are the terms "discipleship" and "apostolate" understood in this chapter, and how do they relate to each other?

2. What would be examples, from your experience, of a lack of "congruence" in the way that the church carries out its calling to be, say, and do witness to the gospel?

3. Paul admonishes the Romans, "Do not be conformed to this world, but be transformed by the renewing of your minds, so that you may discern what is the will of God—what is good and acceptable and perfect" (Rom. 12:2). In what ways do you find that our church is "conformed to this world"?

4. Now that North America, like Europe, has obviously become a mission field, what are the lessons we can learn from the history of modern foreign mission surveyed in this chapter?

5. Why is it often so difficult for our congregations to understand what it means to "exhibit the kingdom of heaven to the world"?

7

Kingdom Exhibition as Witness: Incarnational Formation

The wording of the sixth Great End of the church contains ambiguity that is theologically instructive. The term *End* can mean both "purpose" and "outcome." In their setting in the *Book of Order* of the Presbyterian Church (U.S.A.), the *ends* define the "purposes" of the church.[1] With this statement, we are confessing that the church's *purpose* is to proclaim the gospel, to shelter and nurture the children of God, to maintain divine worship, to preserve the truth, to promote social righteousness, and to exhibit the kingdom of heaven to the world. When they are expressed this way as verbs, these purposes are dynamic, ongoing activities. But their formulation as verbal nouns in our text (proclamation, shelter, maintenance, preservation, promotion, exhibition) might create the impression that these are finished accomplishments of the church. These verbal nouns can seem to imply a static, unchanging character of the church. That is a dimension of the misunderstanding of the church's calling that accompanies the solidity and durability of the Christendom structures we have inherited. Just as the great stone churches of Europe often appear to us as an unchanging and immovable presence in the midst of a rapidly changing world, our thinking and speaking about the church can convey the expectation that the church is the one institution in our society that will not change. In fact, for many church members in North America who are deeply troubled by the rapid changes in our context, it has become very important to preserve the church as the one thing that has not and will not change.

Such thinking easily pollutes a proper biblical sense of the church's calling and purpose. The Great Ends cannot be understood as the perfections of the church. Our proclaiming, nurturing, maintaining, preserving, promotion, or exhibiting are not yet what God has called them to be. We are a church in the process of becoming. Reformed Christians have always been insistent that we are not the church perfected but the church becoming. For that reason, one of the most definitive statements about our tradition has focused on our reality as the *ecclesia reformata semper reformanda secundum verbum Dei*. We are the "church once reformed and always being reformed in accordance with the word of God." This understanding of our reality helps us to practice what Professor Will Storrar calls the "chastened humility" of the church. It helps us to live in the essential and challenging tension of genuine *modesty* on the one hand, because we are not yet what we ought to be and most certainly will be one day, and *conviction* on the other, because our calling is to proclaim the gospel and preserve the truth.

In that sense, the Great Ends point toward the Great Outcomes of the church's pilgrimage. We live in the confidence that the one "who began a good work among [us] will bring it to completion by the day of Jesus Christ" (Phil. 1:6). With Paul, we pray that our "love may overflow more and more with knowledge and full insight to help [us] to determine what is best, so that in the day of Christ [we] may be pure and blameless" (Phil. 1:9–10). We certainly know that we, as one part of the church of Jesus Christ, are not "pure and blameless" now, nor have we ever been. The church has always been a community of forgiven sinners—like that field of wheat and weeds Jesus described in his parable in Matthew 13. But that does not reduce us to despair precisely because God is faithful; God will complete what God has begun; God will bring in the great harvest; and God's Spirit is given to the church to enable her obedience in spite of and in tension with her sinfulness.

In terms of the sixth Great End, this reminds us that our "exhibition of the kingdom of heaven to the world" is not the claim that the church either is or has the blueprints for the kingdom of God. We dare not continue the heresy that equates the church (however defined) with the kingdom of God! Rather, exhibition as witness points toward the promised kingdom for which we pray and which God is bringing to its harvest. This is the reason that we have constantly translated the biblical message with the words "the in-breaking reign of God." We are claiming that in Christ, God's reign is already present and active. "All authority in heaven and on earth has been given to me," announces Jesus to the disciples when he meets them on the Galilean mountain after Easter (Matt. 28:18). We are claiming that, in the life and practices of the witnessing church, this reign is becoming visible, is being enfleshed, and can really be encountered. We are inviting all those to whom we are sent to join us in the pilgrimage of witness that points both to what God has already done in Christ, what God most certainly will do when all things are brought to consummation, and therefore what God is doing now in our midst.

The New Testament places the dynamic of kingdom witness within the work of the Holy Spirit, making it very clear that the in-breaking of the kingdom is not our project but God's. It is the promised Spirit who enters into the waiting community at Pentecost and empowers Peter to proclaim the gospel on behalf of the entire community. It is the Holy Spirit who allows the Ethiopian eunuch to read the prophetic scroll and to sense the truth that is there if someone will explain it to him. It is the Holy Spirit who guides the Roman centurion to pray to the God of the Jews and who directs him to send for Peter. The apostolic missionaries understood that the yield of their witness was the result of the Spirit's work in listening and responding people, not the result of their persuasiveness. As Newbigin summarized it, " . . . the Spirit is the foretaste, the pledge, the *arrabon* [down-payment or earnest] of the kingdom . . . it is a real gift now, a real foretaste of the joy, the freedom, the righteousness, the holiness of God's kingdom."[2]

The way in which the exhibition of the kingdom of heaven to the world actually happens, then, is in the formation of the community of faith so that it can be that witness. As Lesslie Newbigin constantly emphasized, the Holy Spirit calls and equips the church to be a sign, a foretaste, an instrument of God's in-breaking rule. The church fulfills its calling when it points beyond itself to what God's love purposes for all creation. The church carries out its mandated witness when it presents to the world evidence of that divine, healing, reconciling, loving rule in its life and practices now. How the community functions before a watching world, how it is formed to be light, leaven, and salt, how it is, does, and says good news—these are all essential to the exhibition of the approaching reign of God.

The purpose of a theological statement like the Great Ends of the Church is ultimately formative. It is a confessional response to God's calling, putting in words that we, in our years of grappling with that calling, have come to understand about who we are and what we are for. As we focus on what these Great Ends mean in this series of study booklets, we are opening ourselves to the Spirit's shaping power, so that these purposes and outcomes might also characterize our present reality more and more. We shall be more accessible to the Spirit's work in us and through us as we make such formation for witness the central focus of our life together.

It is, however, crucial for this formation that we constantly acknowledge how much formation still needs to be done. We must be transparently honest about our need to "be reformed in accordance with the Word of God." Our witness, as we just pointed out, needs to convey both the modesty and the conviction of a community of forgiven, hopeful, realistic, and confident Christians. There is a necessary dynamic of movement and change that inheres in a witnessing community that knows that it is conformed to the world but also being transformed by God's renewing of its mind (Rom. 12:2). It is for this reason that I have described the formation of the missional church as "the continuing conversion of the church."[3]

The basic principle of the dynamic formation of the community so that it will exhibit the kingdom of heaven to the world is this: *Kingdom exhibition happens as kingdom apostolate emerging from kingdom discipleship.* This basic principle reiterates in summary form what we have been seeking to say about the meaning and practice of the sixth Great End. As disciples of Christ, we learn and experience the message of God's in-breaking reign. This is the theological center of the gathered life of the church. Everything that we do as the assembled community should be an engagement with the Christ who is present when we gather so that we can be formed and equipped by him for the mission to which he calls us. The second, third, and fourth Great Ends are all fundamental dimensions of our formation in the community of faith. The shelter, nurture, and spiritual fellowship of the children of God, the maintenance of divine worship, and the preservation of the truth must all be happening in our community, if we are going to be equipped for the proclamation of the gospel for the salvation of humankind, the promotion of social righteousness, and the exhibition of the kingdom of heaven to the world.

The biblical authenticity of these gathered practices is tested, however, by their necessary relationship to our apostolate. Although there is a necessary internal focus to these Great Ends they are not "ends in themselves." In isolation from missional vocation, these practices become spiritually stagnant and ultimately a betrayal of our calling. The gathered practices of the community of disciples form them together and individually for their apostolate, their sending, their mission. The disciples of Jesus were in training to become apostles, and that continues to be the basic pattern of the apostolic church: discipleship equipping for apostolate, and apostolate enabled, empowered, encouraged, and commissioned by the discipled community. All the Great Ends of the Church are summarized by our Lord's commissioning promise: "You shall be my witnesses."

This means that the practices that exhibit the in-breaking kingdom of heaven to the world are learned within the community of faith, in all the ways that discipling happens. It happens in gathered worship, in hearing and responding to the Word proclaimed and expounded, in sacramental celebration of the concrete reality of the gospel at work in our lives, in the disciplines of spiritual formation, in the diverse expressions of Christian fellowship, in the community's hospitality, and in its mutual forgiveness and reconciliation. All of these practices are formed as the community submits to the discipling power of the biblical Word.

If *kingdom exhibition happens as kingdom apostolate emerging from kingdom discipleship*, then the life and actions of the members of a congregation when they are not gathered is the essential expression of their apostolate. This kingdom exhibition emerges every Sunday as the members of the congregation depart into their respective mission fields. This sixth Great End is, in effect, the theological basis for our understanding of lay witness. Kingdom apostolate is the faithful witness of Christians in the enormous diversity of their distinctive mission fields, Monday through Saturday. As we move away from understandings of the church as places that meet our religious needs, toward a deeply rooted sense of our vocation as God's missionary people, then our members will enter into their daily lives with an articulate sense of sentness. This will be articulate, because it has been the pervasive thrust of the discipling life of the congregation. All of their shared practices will, in some way, focus on the sending that expresses every Christian's baptismal vocation to be a witness for Christ. Because of their discipleship for apostolate, they can live a life of witness in the confidence of God's presence with them. They will be alert to the work of the Spirit around them and preparing for them. They will know that they are not alone: Christ is with them, and they are supported, prayed for, encouraged, and equipped by the sending congregation of which they are a part. They will understand that their Christian witness is not merely particular things that they might say or do (or neglect to say or do) but that it is who they are, everything they do, and everything they say.

They will return to that community of discipleship in order to be equipped anew for their apostolate. That equipping will take place in many ways. It will include listening to each other, encouraging each other, correcting each other, supporting each other, praying for each other, weeping and laughing with each other. It is in this pattern of "inhalation" and "exhalation" of the witnessing community that the kingdom of heaven is exhibited to the world. For kingdom apostolate to emerge from such discipleship, it must focus on the powerful work of the biblical word to form God's people for their missional vocation.

This is the second principle for the formation of the community: *Kingdom exhibition is formed by the missional engagement of the scriptural witness.* Discipleship is the process of "going to the school of Jesus." As we have said, this is the basic pattern of formation laid out in the four Gospels. Following in the tradition of the first disciples, we are enabled by these Scriptures to enter into their school of missional formation. With them, we "learn Jesus." We watch what he does. We hear what he says. We imitate him as he teaches us how to pray. We observe how he deals with the great diversity of people and challenges that he encounters. We learn from him to interpret the great story of God's self-disclosure as the powerful event of God's love bringing about salvation. As the Holy Spirit opens our minds and hearts to the formative Word of God, we discover that we are, in fact, being transformed by the renewing of our minds, just as the disciples experienced with Jesus.

There are many ways to read and interpret Scripture. We are arguing here that the key interpretive approach to the Bible focuses on the apostolic strategy in the first generations of the Christian movement. That strategy was the formation of communities to carry out Jesus' mandate that the witness should expand to embrace not only Jerusalem, Judea, and Samaria, but the "ends of the earth" (Acts 1:8). We learn about this especially in Luke–Acts, but we see evidence of it all through the New Testament. The first missionaries formed communities and equipped them to continue as a witness to the gospel of Jesus Christ. The missionaries typically moved on, trusting God's Spirit to continue that formation. And they wrote to their communities. Their written documents became the New Testament, all of which was oriented toward the continuing formation of missional churches. This was happening in a great diversity of ways, because the challenges and problems of these missional communities were so diverse. But the thrust of their formation centered on their faithfulness as witnessing communities.

If the scriptural word is going to form the community for its apostolate, then the community will need to make such scriptural formation its priority. This calls for difficult decisions regarding time, schedules, and programs. It is not possible for a community of believers to be discipled for their diverse apostolates in a one-hour worship service with a fifteen-minute exposition of the Word of God, once a week. A community's "being transformed by God's renewing of its mind" (Rom. 12:2) is arduous and demanding. The process of apostolic formation takes time and hard work. Peter's first admonition to the congregations to which he addressed his first epistle was, in the wording of the King James Bible, to "gird up the loins of your mind" (1 Pet. 1:13). The image is taken from the athletic world. It has to do with stripping down for hard physical labor—"to put on the jogging suit of your mind." Before any of the great themes of grace, holiness, growth, and purpose can be explored further, Peter's congregations have to grasp the urgency and priority of their mental formation for their calling. The demands of the apostolate are daunting and even impossible if the witnesses are not discipled properly, that is, not fully equipped by the powerful Word of God in the Bible.

In today's world of overfilled schedules and conflicting demands, the requirements of scriptural formation are a telling challenge. One of the first ways that a congregation will reveal that its "missional conversion" may be happening will be their willingness to ask hard questions and make hard decisions about the time it will take for their scriptural formation. These decisions will have their bearing on many aspects of the community's life. It will mean that we reclaim the office of "teaching elder," so that our biblically schooled ministers can concentrate on what their congregations most need: solid, disciplined, honest engagement with the Bible, for the sake of their formation for their apostolic calling. It will also mean that the teaching elder learns how to interpret the Scriptures missionally. There is growing awareness of this need among biblical scholars and many pastors. But there is also a great need to rethink how we learn and teach Scripture if we are going to start with the assumption that its purpose is the missional discipling of the congregation for its apostolate: the exhibition of the kingdom of heaven to the world! There is a parallel need for teaching resources for congregations that will guide them into the wonderful and challenging ways in which the biblical world really does work as the Spirit's instrument for missional formation.

Of course, to set such priorities for the gathered life of a faith community will mean that some other things we would like to do may no longer be our priority. The rapidly changing context within which we now carry out our mission will force us to ask ourselves, "What is most needful, given the time and resources we have, and the urgent challenges of our mission field?" We will have to grapple with conflicts that arise because there will still be expectations about the ways a congregation should "meet my needs." How congregations deal with such conflict will also be an example of the process of exhibiting the kingdom of heaven to the world.

Perhaps our thinking about our gathered life, and its formative purpose, could be helpfully challenged if we paid more attention to the New Testament synagogue as our model. Many biblical scholars and early church historians concur that the Jewish synagogue was the primary model for the emerging life of the apostolic communities. The emphasis of the synagogue was schooling: the learning of the faith and the exploration of the implications of faith for all areas of life. There is a close parallel between such synagogal schooling and the patterns of discipling we learn from Jesus' interactions with the disciples. We have tended, through the course of Christendom, to replace the synagogue with the temple. Early Christian *leitourgia*, the work of the people, has tended to become the liturgy which is the work of the small caste of professional Christians, conducted in great temples that have become ends in themselves. It might be timely to question these cultural adaptations from a synagogue mind-set to a temple and cathedral pattern. Certainly the Reformed tradition, with its emphasis on biblical study, the theologically trained pastorate and ruling eldership, and the teaching of the faith, already positions us in a synagogal trajectory.

The way in which discipleship for apostolate happens is crucial to the community's witness. The practices of biblical formation need to show the congruence between message and method that we defined as "incarnational." There is a further principle of formation for kingdom exhibition that speaks to this issue of incarnational integrity. *Kingdom exhibition happens as the congregation leads its life worthy of the calling to which it has been called* (see Eph. 4:1). This theme is basic to Paul's continuing formation of his congregations. It is constantly repeated in various ways in his epistles:

> As you know, we dealt with each one of you like a father with his children, urging and encouraging you and pleading that you lead a life worthy of God, who calls you into his own kingdom and glory. (1 Thess. 2:11–12)

> To this end we always pray for you, that our God will make you worthy of his call and will fulfill by his power every good resolve and work of faith. (2 Thess. 1:11)

For this reason, since the day we heard it, we have not ceased praying for you and asking that you may be filled with the knowledge of God's will in all spiritual wisdom and understanding, so that you may lead lives worthy of the Lord, fully pleasing to him, as you bear fruit in every good work and as you grow in the knowledge of God. (Col. 1:9–10)

Only, live your life in a manner worthy of the gospel of Christ. (Phil. 1:27)

I therefore, the prisoner in the Lord, beg you to lead a life worthy of the calling to which you have been called. (Eph. 4:1)

This "worthiness" is exhibited in the congruence of the community's life and actions with the message it shares. It is how the congregation witnesses to the fact that in Christ, God's kingdom is now breaking in to human history. This explains the constant emphasis of the apostles on the integrity of the community's life, as we have explored earlier. There is to be a visible correspondence between what we profess and how we live. The vernacular version of this fundamental missional principle puts it simply: We are called to walk our talk. As that happens, the kingdom of heaven is being exhibited to the world.

The biblical formation of the congregation will unpack all the ways that such worthy living happens. It will explore the challenges facing the first Christian congregations, and how the apostles addressed them. It will discover that the problems of the early Christians are very much our problems. As those early Christians tried to sort out how to translate the gospel worthily into their immediate mission fields, we will learn with them what "contextualization" both is and is not. And as we begin to understand more deeply and comprehensively just what this worthiness looks like, we will be equipped to tackle honestly the compromises and reductionisms of our Christendom conditioning.

These discoveries will grow out of the community's shared labors with the biblical word. They cannot be imposed from above. They must be a work of the Holy Spirit that is validated by the growing consensus within the community. As we just said, this does not happen quickly. The conversion of deeply rooted attitudes and assumptions is not often instantaneous, but is rather a process of learning, questioning, testing, and risking. Because this process engages themes and convictions that are important to people, there will be disagreement and conflict as we explore together what worthy living looks like. Then the worthiness of our life will be evidenced in how we learn to disagree Christianly. It will be seen in our readiness to wait and pray for a consensus when the disagreements seem irreconcilable. The exhibition of the in-breaking kingdom of heaven is also happening where Christians learn to forgive each other seventy seven times!

The exhibition of the kingdom of heaven, finally, is to be directed to the whole world. We have focused our discussion on the particular community of faith. This has been intentional, because the particular community, or local congregation, is the primary instrument of God's mission in the world. That conviction is a theological and missiological consensus that is broadly subscribed to. But every local congregation is by definition a part, a member, of the body of Christ that spread around the world and across the generations. Every local congregation represents the church of Jesus Christ to its particular setting. Although no particular company of Christians perfectly embodies the people God calls us to be, every such company bears within it the fullness of the gospel and its missional mandate. Every congregation in every cultural context is both called and enabled to live out the missional pattern of discipleship and apostolate; God's Holy Spirit makes this possible, and the Scriptures are the primary instrument for its realization. The unity of the church is fundamentally the oneness of its message, its mandate, its apostolic mission. And that one mandate is carried out in the almost infinite diversity of particular communities that incarnate the gospel in human cultures. *Kingdom exhibition happens as the sole lordship of Jesus Christ is practiced in the cultural and organizational diversity of the global movement of God's Spirit.*

Early in our discussion, we emphasized that the sovereignty of Christ did not fit worldly patterns of power and might. And yet, it is the expression of God's universal rule! It is in all of heaven and all of the earth that Jesus has been given all power. How shall we understand the exhibition of the kingdom of heaven to all the world without falling into the trap of human conceptions of power and rule? Mustn't Jesus become some kind of universal emperor to make it all work? Can the universal claims of the kingdom be congruent with the gospel of healing and reconciliation, of servanthood and submission, of the cross's scandal and foolishness?

This question has become an urgent one because, as we reviewed above, the Christian movement has, in fact, become a global reality in the last two centuries. What was still in 1900 a movement whose majority was located in the old established "Christian cultures" of

Christendom has radically shifted in the course of a century. By 2000, over 70 percent of the world's Christian population was located outside the boundaries of Western Christendom! As already noted, the church's center of gravity has shifted from the north to the south. In that process, the emerging churches of this global movement have discovered the freedom to shape themselves as witnessing communities that can translate the gospel in their own contexts.

This has not happened easily. There has been resistance to giving up the established patterns of Western Christianity brought by the first missionaries, both on the part of those who were sent and those to whom they were sent. In working through these issues, Christian communities have discovered again and again how the New Testament churches grappled with similar issues.

The Jewish Christians in Jerusalem had to come to terms with the Gentile extension of the church. This unexpected movement into the European, Gentile world, under Paul's leadership, led to the formation of churches that claimed to be an authentic response to the gospel but did not adopt the cultural patterns of faithful Judaism. This was as shocking for the church in Jerusalem as was the formation of a Samaritan church or the conversion of a eunuch. The oldest Christian community had to learn what "living worthy of its calling" meant over against such challenges. For that to happen, Peter had to be converted through his encounter with Cornelius, and Paul had to debate long and hard both in his epistles and in encounters with his Christian brothers in Jerusalem. Ultimately the church had to meet and work out a consensus as recorded in Acts 15. The process depicted there is a concrete model of "worthy living" in a passage of conflict. The scriptural witness to these struggles continues today to be the Spirit's tool to form a global church of ever-growing cultural diversity for its faithful witness.

The emergence of the global church has been accompanied by a growing recognition that such genuine cultural diversity within the church was intended from the beginning. The communication of the gospel in all the languages present in Jerusalem at Pentecost was programmatic for the global extension of the witnessing church. In the Great Commission, Jesus commanded the disciples, now graduating into apostles, to "disciple the nations." It would be more accurate to translate this, "disciple the ethnicities." It implies that the entire process of discipleship formation leading to apostolate, which has been the theological program of Matthew's Gospel, can and should be translated and embodied in any and every ethnic context of the world. The purpose of the Christian mission is not to create a culturally uniform organization around the world. It is, rather, to evoke a multicultural chorus of missional congregations, praising God and witnessing to the gospel in ways that will make this good news known and knowable everywhere. This is how the universal scope of the kingdom of heaven is exhibited: not in some kind of hierarchy of power, but in the harmony of Christian communities in diverse cultures implementing our Great Ends in ways worthy of the gospel, wherever they are.

This worthiness necessarily includes cultural translation. The calling to which we are called is implemented as we experience the Spirit empowering us to cross cultural boundaries and form witnessing communities. Their mission, then, is to continue their witness to the unique gospel event of Jesus Christ, just as this was the purpose of congregations from Antioch to Ephesus, to Athens, to Rome. But they are to do so in new and different languages, with different cultural expressions, forming new and different ecclesial structures. Apostolicity means the freedom of the Christian movement to take root and grow in every distinctive soil on earth. But what is grown from those diverse soils is the same story, the same good news, the witness to the same Lord Jesus Christ.

The multicultural, multiorganizational church exhibits the kingdom of heaven to the world when, in all the diverse ways the story is told, its message is one message. Its way of doing what it does may differ; but basically, witnessing communities centered on the same good news demonstrate it with the same basic practices. All faith communities gather to worship, to praise, to pray, to hear and proclaim Scripture, to respond with confession of faith and the sharing of gifts and resources. All faith communities practice the welcoming hospitality of the loving Father. They all, in their own languages, are discipled by the stories of Jesus in the Gospels and are formed as communities by the epistles. There is no holy language in which the gospel must be shared. Rather, the history can be translated, carried over one cultural barrier after another. And as that happens, the witness spreads "so that grace, as it extends to more and more people, may increase thanksgiving, to the glory of God" (2 Cor. 4:15).

The integrity, congruence, and unity of Christian witness around the world are expressed not by uniform systems of governance and office, nor by one creed subscribed to by all, nor by liturgies and hymnody that are everywhere the same. There will be diverse ways that Christian communities organize themselves. They will write creeds in widely differing contexts, so that their emphases will vary from one instance to the next. Their liturgies will grow out of the incarnation of the gospel in particular cultures, finding language and imagery and poetry that communicate the gospel authentically and understandably for a particular culture. In all of that diversity, however, the event of Jesus Christ is continuing. People are baptized into his name and mission and incorporated into his fellowship. The Lord's Table is celebrated with an infinite variety of breads and wines that convey its truth to diverse cultural contexts. In all of them, Jesus' death is proclaimed until he comes again. The risen Lord is acclaimed and followed, and other, competing gods and powers are rejected. As the power of the gospel grows, and as people are transformed by the renewal of their minds so that they are no longer conformed to their worlds, the conversion of the church continues. This choir whose harmony is made up of infinitely diverse voices sings one truth: "There is one body and one Spirit, just as you were called to the one hope of your calling, one Lord, one faith, one baptism, one God and Father of all, who is above all and through all and in all" (Eph. 4:4–6). When the watching world sees and hears that one message attested by disciples in every ethnicity, then the kingdom of heaven is being exhibited to the world.

Notes

1. This discussion revisits the discussion of "ends," "goals," and "outcomes," in Catherine G. González, introduction to the first book in this series, *Proclamation of the Gospel for the Salvation of Humankind*, pp. 1ff.
2. Lesslie Newbigin, *Mission in Christ's Way* (Geneva: WCC Publications, 1987), pp. 16–17; see also Lesslie Newbigin, *The Open Secret: An Introduction to the Theory of Mission* (Grand Rapids: Wm. B. Eerdmans, 1995), p. 58.
3. Darrell L. Guder, *The Continuing Conversion of the Church* (Grand Rapids: Wm. B. Eerdmans, 2000).

Questions for Reflection and Discussion

1. There is a broad consensus within global Christianity that the local congregation is the primary instrument of God's mission. All six Great Ends of the Church center on the purpose and formation of the local congregation. How does your congregation define its calling? How are the six Great Ends of the Church reflected in your life and ministry?

2. How does the gathered life of your congregation prepare your members for their witness when they are scattered in the world?

3. What are the role and importance of scriptural formation in the life of your congregation?

4. How would a congregation know that it was leading its shared life "worthy of the calling with which it has been called"?

5. How is the setting of your congregation changing, and how does your congregation relate to those changes?

A Basic Bibliography for the Study of the Theme of the Kingdom of God

Arias, Mortimer. *Announcing the Reign of God: Evangelization and the Subversive Memory of Jesus.* Lima, OH: Academic Renewal Press, 2001.

Bright, John. *The Kingdom of God: The Biblical Concept and Its Meaning for the Church.* Nashville: Abingdon-Cokesbury Press, 1953.

Castro, Emilio. *Freedom in Mission: The Perspective of the Kingdom of God: An Ecumenical Inquiry.* Geneva: World Council of Churches Publications, 1985.

Fuellenbach, John. *Church: Community for the Kingdom.* Maryknoll, NY: Orbis Books, 2002.

Fuellenbach, John. *The Kingdom of God: The Message of Jesus Today.* Maryknoll NY: Orbis Books, 1995.

Henderson, Robert T. *Joy to the World: An Introduction to Kingdom Evangelism.* Atlanta: John Knox Press, 1980.

Küng, Hans. *The Church.* Trans. Ray and Rosaleen Ockenden. London: Burns & Oates, 1967.

Lohfink, Gerhard. *Jesus and Community: The Social Dimension of Christian Faith.* Trans. J. P. Galvin. Philadelphia: Fortress Press, 1984.

Newbigin, Lesslie. *Sign of the Kingdom.* Grand Rapids: Wm. B. Eerdmans, 1980.

Paul, Robert S. *Kingdom Come!* Grand Rapids: Wm. B. Eerdmans, 1974.

Ridderbos, Herman N. *The Coming of the Kingdom.* Trans. H. de Jongste. Philadelphia: Presbyterian and Reformed Pub. Co., 1962.

Snyder, Howard A. *Models of the Kingdom.* Nashville: Abingdon Press, 1991.